This book is dedicated to my tiny Despair Junior, without whom I would be pointless.

INTRODUCTION

Welcome, dear reader... adventurer in the brackish waters of the future.

You hold in your hands/stumps/mechanical-gripping-fronds the FINEST COMPENDIUM OF WISDOM that has ever graced this woe-begotten planet. The knowledge that suffuses these pages has taken a most circuitous route, but do not doubt for a second that it has in any way been watered down. Like a delicious, lemon-flavoured drink made at four in the morning with the last of the vodka and something from a mostly green bottle, these truths are bitter, yet must be imbibed.

"Tell me more about the origin of this dense, inescapable, occasionally erotic intelligence that I clasp, tremulously!" I hear you cry! (I hear it, even if you did not cry it. And in hearing it, I make you cry it. Such is the force of my hearing). Oh yes, I hear it. And regardless, I'm going to tell you.

For these words have come via quantum-entanglement, stellar radiation and (on more than one occasion) things I found written in cack on the back of rusty white vans parked near my local. Their origin is plain: the nebulous, terrifying, alien EQUINE INTELLECTS that lurk majestically almost a universe's in distance from our pitiful globe.

Some say they materialised beyond the dark star EL SANGUADOR (it IS a star, I can show you where it is). Other fools place the DARK ZONE as somewhere adjacent to the Rhomboid Dimensions. Those people are twats. And they do not wash. And they watch Sky News and consider it well-researched. Seriously.

Many have pondered the origin of these truths and in doing so have fatally sprained their minds. Even those of sufficiently powerful intellects shudder at the task.

It has been studied by those possessed of the SEVENTH GRADE OF FORESIGHT (granted only to the handful who can remain powerfully erect while watching the SQUATINOUS PORN GOATS of ULTRA-WOLVERHAMPTON dance their globular gyrations).

All that was found of their remains was a delicious strawberry blancmange. Since that time, most have shunned its consideration.

Now that you are convinced of the self-evidence of The Truths, you will be reassured to hear of their journey.

Indeed, The Truths wound their way across the distance, unstoppable and intended for one true destination - the mind of the Deliverer, He Who Will Unburden Himself Mightily, the Great That'll Learn You-er, The Chap Who Once Met Big Kev (second tallest bloke in the Spa, Burntwood, Staffordshire), El Guapo Extremo! Le seul vrai roi de Bognor Regis!

Me, dear friends. That one is me. I have the honour to shoulder that burden.

"AND WHO ARE YOU? THAT NAMES HIMSELF THUS AND STANDS HERE GOING ON LIKE A TOOL FOR QUITE SOME TIME, NOW?"

What? Back off! Sit down. Put your trousers back on. This is a family pub.

I am nobody. I am simply the voice that guides. AND YET, I AM EVERY WOMAN, IT'S ALL IN ME.

Some call me "Chaka Khan". Some, "Bernard the Talking Pelvis". Others yet name me "Get Out of my House, You're Tangibly Not My Uncle".

I answer to all of these names, but only one truly fits me.

I am Doctor Despair...

- and these are my HORRORSCOPES.

THANKS

Doctor Despair would like to thank...

For encouragement and kindess throughout this journey into the dark heart of man: John Cartwright, Jessamy Barker, Benjamin James and Jonathan Stilts must be honoured. Their names will be carved at the base of the 200ft tall iron penis that stands at the gates of the Poorly Hidden City on Phallus Five.

For enthusiasm and his most wonderful depiction of my cruel and diabolical visage, Kris Turvey (Lord of the Dark Places and Majestic Sex Warrior of the Fourth Dimension) must receive dire tribute.

In recognition of her inspiration and tolerance, platitudes and an offering of obscene Chinese fruits are placed at the altar of Jodi Crisp, Mistress of Low Twickenham (and Defender of Cheam).

Finally, we invoke the mighty Paul Lamb, Emperor of the Vortex of Thrungos IX (whose seven nipples control the destiny of galaxies) and genuflect in gratitude for his numerous literary boons.

The Doctor would love to thank these people most sincerely. Truly, he would.

But due to a necromancer, he cannot.

HOW TO USE THIS GRIMOIRE

This tome comprises readings for fifty-two of your Earth 'weeks'. In addition to this, there is a section for each of the star signs, describing the general personalities of each sign and salient information about their lives (what they like or dislike, how to court such a person, etc).

There is no truly correct way to read this book - for in reality, it reads you. As your eyes stroke the page, so the inky words reach back into your retina and lick your brain. I do not exaggerate, they're doing it right now. An awkward feeling, is it not? Indeed. But such is the price we must pay to receive the very wisdom contained herein.

These near-sentient puddles of word soup are imbued with a power beyond human comprehension, such that they will form the exact sentences the reader required at the time of their reading, rather than (as in less auspicious publications) requiring the reader themselves to search for a particular date or section. Perhaps you will not find the information that you seek, but you will most certainly receive the information you need. The Terrifying Horse Minds from Just Next to Scrunthos IX are very clear on this issue. The last time I questioned them about it, I was punished with a week-long ice-cream headache and I am seriously not going back there again, girlfriend.

And so! You may search for the reading of the week of the year in which you currently find yourself! Certainly, you may. But just as equally, you may take the book and throw it in the air, catching it upon your strangely dextrous nipples and simply gorge upon the textual sweetmeats you find before you, trusting to fate (and the aforementioned Terrifying Horse Minds). All will be well. Or, in any case, equally horrific.

It is important to know that all of the information contained in this volume is 100% accurate and has been verified under the most extreme scrutiny of a chap wot I met in a hedge. The chap was extremely knowledgeable and I have no reason to doubt the veracity of his assessment. Nor should you.

Proceed, now, knowing that you hold in your hands (or unusually dextrous nipples) the single source of absolute truth to be found in this universe.

MAY THE HORSE BE WITH YOU.

ALWAYS.

READINGS

1

The week of January the 1st

Good evening, dear reader. Or morning. Or noon. Look, forget it. I'm an all-seeing, prescient, time-travelling fortune teller, not a weather girl.

The position of your sun is immaterial to me, particularly given that next week, it's getting... ah, but that would give the game away. Let us begin.

∾

Aries: Why waste time pondering the imponderables? You already have the answers you need - thinking it over and over, turning it around in your mind like an unsolvable Rubiks cube is mere self-flagellation that will lead to no boon. The facts are self-evident. She left you because you are a ridiculous pervert. You'll win her back because you get shoes at half price.

Taurus: Bulls, man! Bulls! Who likes bulls? They're huge, they stink, they wreck the place. I mean, seriously, it's ridiculous. You come in and you're wearing the hat and you've got the threads and she's all, like

"Sorry, dude, I'm riding outta here on some bulls" as if that makes any kind of sense. You get back home to your crib and DAMN, bulls drank all your soup, left the place looking like an explosion in a freakshow. BULLS. Why they got to play it that way? Pfft! OK, everyone secretly likes bulls.

Gemini: Your deluxe 25th anniversary gold-plated Knight Rider boxed set will get you through the holidays, but you won't ever be truly satisfied until you own the ceremonial Y-fronts.

Cancer: Decisions, decisions. So often in life, picking the wrong path, flipping the coin just so, can lead either to success or tragedy. This is no exception. Today will bring you great luck if you buy avocados. ONLY avocados. Otherwise, death.

Leo: That poncho looks ridiculous. You can't go out of the house looking like that, seriously. The fit is all wrong. The colours are horrific. And you work at a funeral parlour. On the plus side, though, they can't see what you're doing under it.

Virgo: Some geese are likely to take an unseemly interest in you between 2:30pm and 3:30pm tomorrow. At first you will feel confused, flustered and unsure how to proceed. The stars say: follow your heart, let them have their way. That gander's a smug bastard anyway.

Libra: An interesting time, profoundly subject to the sway of the heavenly bodies swinging into significant configurations over the next few days. As Neptune moves into ascendency, you are drawn to thinking about a change of location. It could be to your benefit if you give this some thought as you... Dude... what are you doing with that helmet? You're not supposed to actually GO to Neptune, that's ridiculous. Even if you do have a surprisingly high-quality home-made space rocket. Wow. You really put some time into that thing, didn't you? Crazy. I don't know, eh? Librans. So literal.

Scorpio: Trouble at the office. Intrigue and politics abound and will complicate your otherwise harmonious environment. Despite your vigilance and attempts to hold a neutral position in most conflicts, you will find yourself inevitably inveigled. Resentment and ill-will breed more of their own. Anyway: your co-workers motives are not to be depended upon - so eat their biscuits while they're not looking.

Sagittarius: Never rub another man's rhubarb.

Capricorn: No. Absolutely not. Nowhere does it read "The path to righteousness is paved with tiny shrew corpses". I don't even know where you got that from. There's something deeply wrong with you, man. I want all that cleaned up.

Aquarius: Love looms in your life, the stars show a strange, powerful magnetism at work that will guide you to the one with whom you are destined to couple. In fact, the stars are extremely specific about this: the next green-grocer you make eye contact with shall bed you and accompany you to heights of sexual athleticism you previously considered illegal. Ding dong!

Pisces: Whatever you're thinking about doing with

that drill, put it down and eat your dinner.

~

The time has come! Or is behind us! It is passed, and yet lies in wait.

It surrounds us, yet we touch it not.

It is inside us and fills us deeply, which is disconcerting and more than a little suggestive.

In these ways (and others), the time is very much like a cucumber.

Farewell.

2

The week of January the 8th.

Crystal balls! Tea-leaves! The casting of the yarrow stalks!

Forget that pointless guff and get a load of me...

~

Aries: Awful news! Mars is in conjunction with Jupiter today, governing finance - this bodes remarkably ill for your tech industry shares! SELL NOW! SELL IT ALL! ROCK BOTTOM PRICES, IT MUST ALL GO!

Taurus: Hahahah! I totally lied to those credulous Aries gonks! If I were you, I'd put in a call to my broker right now and buy all their stocks at some seriously tasty prices while they're running around, crapping themselves. We'll clean up! Result like that deserves a bevvy, I reckon! Mine's a Dom Perignon. Cheers!

Gemini: Good gravy, those ridiculous Taureans are gullible muppets. They swallowed it hook, line, sinker and copy of the Angling Times, I reckon. If you want to shift that crate of Dom Perignon, now's the time. Know what I mean? You can owe me. Regards to your old dear. See you at the club.

Cancer: It is prudent to maintain a baseline awareness of one's environment at all time, lest she be surprised by an undetected turn of events. Or, as they say in Cheam, "A wise man checks his crisps for spiders when his nephews are visiting for the weekend." Especially that one with the glasses. Nasty little sod.

Leo: Stay calm, concentrate, you can do this. Now: make a small incision below the left ventricle, cutting down toward the aorta. Good, good, you're doing great. Just keep it together for a few more minutes, then you can get them all sutured up, off the slab and back into recovery. Excellent. You really must revise this stuff for next time, though.

Virgo: That beard's looking fine. Honestly! It's vibrant, it's a statement! Ignore the chap at the service station. What does he know about anything? Sitting there all day, trying to sell people sweets they don't want when they come in to pay for petrol. Not quite knowing what to say, but waggling his eyebrows like a flightless bird when somebody comes in to buy one of the magazines from the top shelf with the young ladies flapping their bits around. Is he some kind of arbiter of fashion in the world today? Not a chance. Still. Might be wise to put some trousers on, though, eh? They have cameras on forecourts, these days.

Libra: Hello! My name is Inigo Montoya. You killed my father. Prepare to die.

Scorpio: Scorpio maaaaan! Scorpio maaaan! Does exactly what a scorpion can! Can he fly? We don't know! Open the window! Wheeeee! No.

Sagittarius: Today, the stars reckon you should put your feet up. Have a lie in, phone in sick and blame it on the snow and the trains. Unless you drive trains - in which case, get work, you lazy cocks.

Capricorn: Politics: Avoid entering a reciprocal tea making arrangement with co-workers, or any other drinks-based barter system. Deals will be broken and long-running feuds will once again be aired. It might be wise to take your own biscuits this week. Keep them secret. Keep them safe.

Aquarius: Love advice from the stars: Today, you would be well-served by adopting the accent and attire of erstwhile 80s hero, Mr T. You will spend the forthcoming week getting in exactly no planes and a considerable amount of your time and energy will be expended in the field of fools (and the pitying thereof). All of this will, however, make you somehow irresistible. The stars don't go into how that works. Sucka.

Pisces: You will meet a tall, dark, handsome stranger. With a drill.

~

Truth disgorged! The ethereal mind-link betwixt us and the nameless horse-minds galloping around the darkest nebulae in the galaxy next-door closes, leaving us alone and adrift once more. Return to your daily dalliances as though nothing happened. Show no sign to those around you that you are any the wiser. Return to the hoi polloi and blend in, just like the rest.

Except of course, now you know.

Oh, now you know.

Also, you've got that massive facial tattoo that says "I KNOW SEECRITS".

Hmmm.

3

The week of January the 15th

BY THE SIX HAIRLESS BALL-BAGS OF HANSON!

Screw your credulity to the sticking post and suspend your disbelief using your strongest, springiest belief-suspenders... you know, the red ones!

Come with me, now, my beautiful little reindeers of the imagination...

~

Aries: Your stars are particularly clear today, making this reading extremely specific. Banjos will feature heavily in today's proceedings. Don't wear the green braces. Beware of tramps, mothers and the letter 'Q'. Avoid the corn. Get the butt-tattoo, it is genius. And finally: DUCK! Phew... close one!

Taurus: Love: Karma lurks, ready to pounce, like a duck in a nightclub (for ducks). Indeed, your philandering past will haunt you today, as you discover that you have somehow managed to make a children's television presenter pregnant. Really, you should know better than this. No matter how arousing it was to have a crack at them while they wore the hippo outfit, you're going to regret not listening when they demanded it in the face.

Gemini: You may not have earned forgiveness, but you seem to have escaped the worst of the consequences. By now, it's probably safe to assume the gypsy has left the area and her curse has worn off. In any event, by the end of the week, it should be safe to touch it again. With iron tongs, that is. Be gentle.

Cancer: Romance: As the Moon obscures Pluto and Venus becomes square, you may find yourself drawn inevitably toward fantasising about lizards. Sexy, sexy lizards. In silk négligées. Wearing bright red lipstick.

Leo: Work: The office is likely to feel quite toxic today. It hasn't escaped your attention that your habit of tea-bagging sleeping colleagues isn't helping matters. At the same time, though, you feel extremely reluctant to stop - at least not until you've flopped them on that dork from marketing. If anyone in the world deserved balls on the chin, that guy does. You'll have to think of some way to diffuse the situation... but that can wait! Looks like somebody's eyelids are feeing heavy...

Virgo: Some days, you've just got to brush your nipples against a badger. Everyone gets that, my friend. Everyone.

Libra: Every silver lining has a cloud. Every rose has its thorn. Every Gallagher family has its Liam. Every bag of Revels has its coffee-cremes. The stars are trying to break it to you gently, OK? It's going to be a "challenging" week. Consider wearing the extra-strong underpants and try to remain within sprinting distance of the lavatory at all times. That's all we can tell you.

Scorpio: Remember, groove *is* in the heart.

Sagittarius: Following an altercation which scares your mother, you will be summarily crowned the Fresh Prince of Bel Air. It is incumbent upon you to travel to the seat of your kingdom forthwith. Though the journey may be arduous, it will afford you time to record the events that have befallen you recently in the oral tradition of your people. Perhaps history will judge the behaviour of those ignominious and uncouth gentlemen to have been fortuitous in the full tapestry of circumstance.

Capricorn: Despite the witnesses, the police report and the mountain of professionally-taken photographic evidence, one thing is certain this week: nobody is going to believe why you killed that fox with a wok. Least of all, Gok Wan. He wants his wok back. He. Is. Livid.

Aquarius: Um Bongo, Um Bongo, dey drink it in de Congo.

Pisces: OK, so you're a dentist, and, OK, they have plaque. It all LOOKS above board, sure. Nonetheless, that is in no way the right drill for the job.

~

These HorrorScopes were brought to you by the wisdom of the DARK STARS OF EL SANGUADOR.

Long may their equine shadows stretch against the face of our pallid planet, steeped in mighty justice and all-encompassing wis— it's OK, actually, they've buggered off.

Arseholes.

4

The week of January the 22nd

Tear up the lifestyle magazine. Sack your therapist. Telephone a random number and scream down the line "YOU KNOW NOTHING!"

But we've got your back. Oh, yes. Pull on your prediction trousers, baby, and slip on your truth jacket. It's time to lap up the milk of your future.

∾

Aries: The stars are feeling a bit vague about you at the moment. Either that or they're just tired. Regardless: Someone in your life that you've liked for a long time will do a thing with someone else and blah blah, diddly doo, skip to the end: you get inexplicably savaged by wolves.

Taurus: Work: Though there are many factors orbiting your professional situation at the moment, much of it may be safely ignored as gossip and speculation. In fact, the only talk around the water-cooler today that you should really pay attention to is likely to revolve around the sudden outbreak of wolves in the office.

Gemini: Introspection beckons, Gemini. You must examine your own motives and recent deeds to discover the truth about your destiny. Take some time to slow down and reflect. Listen to the voice of your heart. A life-affirming rhythm that almost sounds like... wait... howling? barking? ARGH THE WOLVES GOD HELP ME THE WOLVES HOW DID THEY EVEN GET UP HERE INTO THIS TREE HOUSE

Cancer: Success, victory and a well-earned contentment are set to rule your world. Put aside the troubles of today and relax... For you are the Wolf-Lord, and today, your people arise! ArooOOOOoo!

Leo: Add that extra 'zing' to your interpersonal relationships. Make full eye-contact and smile broadly at everybody you meet today. They will think you're absolutely fucking insane.

Virgo: As Mars moves into a sideways configuration with Milton Keynes, your week is going to have the feeling of a near miss. But hey, whatever it was didn't happen! You're looking good, feeling good! Today's going to be amazing! Just... do us a favour and avoid Wolverhampton. If at all possible. No reason.

Libra: Obviously, recent events have taken their toll on you a little and left you performing beneath your best. People will make allowances - nobody's perfect - but still, you feel the need to shake yourself out of this rut. So, what will it be? Maybe a change of diet would perk you up? Buy some new clothes? Get out in the sun more? Have you tried therapy? DRUGS? GOD DAMNIT, I CAN'T SOLVE EVERYTHING! HAVE

YOU TRIED WEARING THE HORSE MASK AND THRASHING IT WITH A FISTFUL OF NETTLES?

Scorpio: Wandering around aimlessly, staring off into space, never really feeling like you're going anywhere. Ah, what are we going to do with you, Scorpio? You know perfectly well what. Now, get back in the box, or you'll get the hose again.

Sagittarius: You will discover a mystical flute with which you'll control the creatures of the woodland. Seriously. No catch.

Capricorn: Love: It's possible you will be posed some awkward decisions by somebody close to you, or that you would like to become more intimate with. The stars advise keeping an open mind. For instance - and this is just an example, but try not to be immediately turned off by her suggestion of a pact with the devil. She *has* got *extremely* pleasant breasts.

Aquarius: Today, you will inexplicably start talking like a rasta. This turns out to be permanent, mon.

Pisces: You're doing great, everyone is proud of you and you should be proud of yourself. Real improvement has been made all round and things are definitely starting to pick up. You've lasted all week without another incident - who would have thought? So, breathe deep. We can do this. Just serve the drinks and smile. You know the drill. Mmmm. Drills.

Hoo, yeah. Seems like we all got caught in a truth-shower there. Looking kinda slippery, right? Oh yeah.

Perhaps you'd best slide on out of those prediction trousers and warm yourself by the fire while I bring us something to... warm you up...

Wait, where are you going?

God damnit.

Another lonely night in the truth-hutch.

5

The week of January the 29th

CLENCH YOUR NIPPLES TIGHTLY IN AN-
TICIPATION!

Fresh wisdom reaches us once more, sleeting
through the heavens from the Equine Intelligences beyond the dark star EL SANGUA-
DOR...

~

Aries: We all like to dress up - don't we? Sure! Of
course we do. And with Easter only a few months
away, now's a good time to dig out your Scooby Doo
outfit and cut out some holes in the appropriate places. Perhaps "appropriate" wasn't exactly the word we
were grasping for there.

Taurus: You're going to have to make a judgement
call on this one. Take a moment to assess the evidence
and come down on one side or the other before people
start to talk. Seriously. It's got to be one thing or the
other. Either this entire restaurant smells of shit... or
you do.

Cancer: Interesting times lie in your path. As we see

in the heavens the majestic arc of Cassiopeia wheeling over head, it is necessary for us to take into consideration the attractive pull of — SHIT SHIT FUCKING LEG IT, KEV, IT'S THE BABYLON! GO ON, JUMP THE FENCE YOU IDIOT JUMP THE BLOODY FENCE ARRGH crap Okay, it's OK. Nah, I just cut myself, I'm fine. Phew. Tell me you didn't throw that joint away? Blimey. Anyway...

Leo: Romance: Come on, Leo, you really must face facts. Once is an accident. Twice, a mistake. Three times, and we're just going to assume you're a little bit dirty.

Virgo: Practical advice from the all-knowing space-horses, this week: Despite your instinct, it is almost never necessary to cover an entire dog in Caramac. Everyone will get the message if you just do the tail.

Libra: Try sleeping at the other end of the bed. To confuse the spiders.

Scorpio: Though they have been troubling you for a long time now, your constantly repeating dreams of American politician Al Gore signify something actually quite simple to explain, that has been staring you in the face all along: You are Al Gore.

Sagittarius: You know what they say, Sagittarius. What's that? You don't know what they say? Ah, well, lucky we're here, then. In your particular circumstances, they say this: Float like a butterfly, sting like a bee, dance like an ocelot, fuck like a bag of rabid stoats.

Capricorn: It's no good. You won't be able to evade the consequences this time. You are totally busted. Turn yourself in before they find you. She put a webcam in the fridge.

Aquarius: Work: It seems like your plans to change career path are well timed. The heavens point to a unique union between Omega 3 (the fish oil constellation) and Bumdisaster Proxima (the one that looks like a pug dog having a seizure), boding well for a change of profession. But, before you leave accountancy for good, they beg you to consider one final action: While nobody's looking, why not replace all the number '9's in every spreadsheet on the network for the word 'Belgium'?

Pisces: No, no, no. I have the official series guide right here, you must have remembered it wrongly. There was never a member of the Justice League of America called "Super Drill". But, OK, I must admit that new cape does rather suit you.

~

Your mind has been upgraded! Congratulations! You will now be able to see things in up to three dimensions, listen to the world in glorious black and white and smell like you've never smelled before! THROUGH TIME!

Now, take it away from this place and inflict it

upon other people.

Don't look at me like that, I ain't the hospitality, I just work here.

~

[edit]: As has been pointed out, Gemini was absent from today's forecast. This was, of course deliberate. This week, Gemini is a roll-over sign, so there will be two predictions next time.

Plus, you know, fuck Gemini.

6

The week of February the 5th

Read and absorb today's HorrorScopes... May they GUIDE YOU and keep you warm inside, like a kind of internal blanket, through what remains of your life. And Beyond...

~

Aries: Community: You are popular with your neighbours and that will stretch a long way. However, this is surely the last time they're going to let you use the "it caught some kind of computer virus" excuse. You simply must find a way to stop your robot daughter from eating those cats. At least in public. It's when she chews on the bones. Ew.

Taurus: So, here we are, eh? An unpleasant week of reaping what we have sown. Still, soon it will be over and life may return to its usual pace. Hopefully you will have learned valuable lessons. Just one small tip, though, while we're chatting... Generally speaking, the judge prefers folks to answer with a simple "Yes, m' lud" over a chirpy "Back once again with the renegade master".

Gemini: You seem to be going about things in a particularly circuitous fashion at the moment. In this particular instance, it seems that your friend's precious guitar will have burned to ashes long before the champagne you're drinking makes its way through your body to be effectively used in the act of fire-fighting. We don't want to jump the gun, but it's almost as though you know this to be the case.

Gemini 2: *(Gemini is a roll-over symbol this week. In a roll-over, you may choose to believe either of the two predictions that you would rather happen. Although the nastier one will definitely happen).* A typographical error causes you be the recipient of 20 melons when you in fact ordered lemons. Inconvenient. The same "mistake" appears to have caught you again when you ordered that large boxed set of Dido's.

Cancer: Step outside of your comfort zone. Forge new relationships. Just once, instead of giving money to a tramp, try giving them a little kiss.

Leo: Love: It isn't always necessary to scrutinise the situation. Don't look for complex answers, go with the feeling. The stars promise that when you look into his eyes, you will understand. That much chest-hair just plain makes a priest horny.

Virgo: Food: We don't want to get into too much detail here (and believe me, we're the stars, we can see - everything - too much, in this instance) However, without getting you all stressed out, you might want to start carrying a jar or mayonnaise with you AT ALL TIMES. Your immediate future contains a LOT more salad than you typically enjoy.

Libra: Take a little "me" time today. Turn off your mobile phone, dim the lights. Allow yourself a glass of aromatic, low-alcohol wine. Some Enya and a light yoghurt, perhaps. Or being brutally sodomized by ten angry greek men. Whatever suits, really.

Scorpio: Oh god. I can barely look. My dear friend, NEVER insult the tattooist.

Sagittarius: This week, the stars have a message for you. Yes, you - personally so. It may seem hard to believe, but it's true. This evening, step out into your back yard (or gaze longingly through the bars of your cell, depending on circumstances) and look upwards to the heaven. What do you see? Can it be? Yes. YES! The clouds part and the bright, shining stars reveal the word... "Pelvis". Literally nothing else, that's your lot. Still. Phwoar, eh? "Pelvis".

Capricorn: A beautifully-written letter will arrive at your abode, enclosed in a pure white envelope that seems to weigh almost nothing and glistens in the moonlit sky. Upon reading the missive, you will discover that you are invited to attend an audience with her majesty, the Queen of the Elves. She demands your presence. She wishes to see you boogie.

Aquarius: Perhaps this week, you will be able to pick up the phone, ask to speak to your mother and cry "HAHAH, IN YOUR FACE, YOU WITCH!" - That's right. Your maths PhD finally proves its worth when you are able to use it to categorically prove that there Ain't No Party like an S-Club Party.

Pisces: Analysis: You dream of spinning, always spinning, plunging into dark holes, spitting sawdust from your teeth. This is normal.

~

With that, the predictions are complete and we may adjourn. Go forth, invigorated by DARK WISDOM, children of the horsepocalypse.

Rear up on your hind legs and whinny into the night!

7

The week of February the 12th

Lost in the rings of Neptune? Out of rocket-fuel and surrounded by Space Ham™? Then it's time for HorrorScopes.

In fact, where the hell have they been? They're late. I'm calling head office about this.

~

Aries: Timing is everything, and mother nature seems to be smiling on you at the moment. The clouds will open, the winds will drop off and for miles around, all will be placid and gentle. All of which suggests that this week would be perfect weather conditions under which to launch your home-made Zeppelin.

Taurus: Food: Try something that scares you every day. Ideally, for lunch. The stars indicate you should daub a dollop of peanut butter on a cracker, add a chunk of sharp cheddar and top it all with a pickled onion. Yow!

Gemini: One day soon, far from home, you will awaken from sleep surrounded by hungry clowns sporting preposterous erections. Though you will not remember anything of the preceding evening - certainly not the location of your clothes or mobile phone... or car - you will at least remember the name of the bikers you apparently spent the evening with, as their names now adorn your arms, chest and face. Also, in some cases, innards.

Cancer: Technology increasingly rules our lives, from the profound to the mundane. Like a kind of digital chaos-theory, a transposed digit in China can mean a hurricane in Kent. Today, to demonstrate this point neatly, a simple HTML error will result in your purchasing a beautiful, full-leather car with aluminium seats.

Leo: Some wisdom transcends the ages: I've said it before and I'll say it again. Never give a gypsy calcium.

Virgo: Time to re-invigorate. Shake it up. Turn the tables. Break the rules. Take a chance. Place a bet. Shave your pubic hair into a mohican. Spit on her grandma. Go on, really moisten the old lass. Show her the mohican. She might be into that. How's she looking? Not so enthused? Yeah, that was a long shot. Probably time to leg it. High-tail it out of town! Hunker down low in a safe house! Wait until nobody remembers you... Then go right back and do it all over again! Woooo! She might like it this time! Yeah! Hahaaa! What? No? Jesus. Okaaaaaay... Time for that career in accountancy. Balls.

Libra: Play it cool. Nobody has to guess about your inner-most urges. You can style it out - you're a pro. Just remember: no matter how guilty you feel, it's very, very unlikely that anyone else will know how deep you've been inside that Poodle.

Scorpio: You combine Kung-Fu and Mung beans. You call it Mung-Fu. You are the world's first Mung-Fu sensei. It is well lethal.

Sagittarius: Romance: Memories of past loves linger on in hearts and minds. When you feel low and reflect on how things went, it's important to know that they feel these things, too. The truth is: it isn't only you that occasionally feels fragile. Even though you're apart, he's still thinking about you. The way you looked when you were happy. The thoughtful moments. And, yes, the time you burned the word "hate" into that dude's ballbag while he was unconscious.

Capricorn: The stars are looking pretty intense for you right now. Almost... fizzy with excitement. Indeed, the challenges ahead of you will be taxing, high-fructose and deeply erotic. For instance, one of the least interesting afternoons of the week ahead sees you being attacked in the street by a gang of highly-skilled lesbian caterers, wielding foot-long marzipan phalluses. They will find you quite delicious.

Aquarius: Things are definitely looking up for you this week. There is an unmistakeable spring in your step and a knowing twinkle in your eye. You feel confident, strong and in control of the moment. Wearing her panties fucking ROCKS, man.

Pisces: Finally, you unplug the drill and wade through the blood to a new tomorrow. A fresh new day whispers: "hammers!"

~

It ends! They are complete, the truths have been unloaded directly into your face and from thence to your frail human minds.

Sleep easily, twisted mortals, for soon I will be with you once more. For now, however, EL SANGUADOR beckons!

8

The week of February the 19th

Fortune, mate! Fortune! Read your fortune? Tell you your fortune for a fiver, sir? Alright, call it a pound! OK, OK, fifty... ten pence! Come on, mate! Just ten pence for your fortune! A bargain, just show us yer hand!

Oh god. Oh, dear sweet god. I ain't never seen a hand like that before, mate, that's bloody disgusting. Get out! Get out and never come back, you pervert!

~

Aries: Politics: This week, as the result of a top-secret ballot, you will be secretly appointed Chancellor of the Exchequer, and held to blame for the state of the economy. This probably seems a little rough, particularly when hundreds of thousands of people turn up at your door, protesting, shouting at you and generally venting their anger. On the up side: free red briefcase. Can't say fairer than that. Bargain.

Taurus: Entertainment: You are stopped in the street by an elderly gentleman dressed as some sort of rapper, who eagerly drags you into a television studio and points a number of broadcast cameras in your face. After being told that you have no 'ride', the confused man from the TV looks around, distraught for a few moments, then, with a look of resignation, sighs and reluctantly pimps your nan.

Gemini: No, no, no, no, no! You're doing it wrong again. How many times must we go over this? You washed the right hand 3 times more than the left. Go back and start again.

Cancer: It is incumbent upon us all to assist in the delivery of justice in our local communities. And so, on this day, it comes unto you. Your good turn for the day will be to locate, stalk and brutally execute a man in a full-body Jar Jar Binks costume. You have your orders. Take him out, ganglands style. (NOT Gangnam Style. You heard.) Bring back the head as proof. You may discard the eyes.

Leo: Long-term plans begin to mature for you after many months of preparation. Finally, just as you had begun to give up on the whole idea, your boss notices you walking without your feigned limp and begins to believe that you are Keyser Söze.

Virgo: You will need to focus on efficiency this week. There are many ways to improve the throughput of an organisation such as yours and great potential for reward if you are able to take a step back and consider things dispassionately. Besides; there's no point in having midget servants if you don't learn to delegate.

Libra: You're too shy. Hush, hush. Eye to eye.

Scorpio: Business: Dress for the job you want, not the job you have. He might be your boss, but he must still learn respect for your pimp hat and cane. Knock out his gold fronts. Oh yeah! Now he crying! Now he crying! Take his damn fool watch offa his wrist and get the sucka's wallet, too! You ain't gonna be buying lunch from Lidl today, no goddamn way!

Sagittarius: When faced with adversity, remember the secret wisdom passed down through the generations, that kept your father's father alive in the darkest of times: Down, down+forward, forward+punch.

Capricorn: The time is right, you can't afford to hesitate a moment longer. Pull on your lab coat. Set up the cage. Go and get your syringe. There has never been a more auspicious day for you to inseminate a Labrador.

Aquarius: The universe can be made to bend to your will. It's true. The correct combination of thoughts and action will bring you your heart's desire immediately and without effort. Focus. Concentrate. Clearly visualise the thing you want most in your life. Make the picture so detailed and realistic in your mind that you could reach forward and take it. Now, bitch-slap the nearest person who has one.

Pisces: All is relaxation and peace. Drink in the tranquility and let it become a part of you. Imagine you are adrift in an ocean of calm. Let the soothing rhythm of enormous hammers wash over you.

~

These words might have come to you for free, but rest assured, they cost somebody somewhere... dearly. Possibly over four Euros.

May they guide and protect you and forever deliver you from Wolverhampton.

9

The week of February the 26th

Ladies. Gentlemen. Obsidian power-fish from the Rhomboid Dimensions: Today, I open my mind to the horse-people!

Pull back your human masks, revealing your true faces. Hook yourself into your glowing pleasure-machines and dial 'Y' for 'YES, SIR, I CAN BOOGIE'.

~

Aries: "Warning: The value of your collection of vintage Mary Poppins pornography can go down as well as up." - Always be sure to read the small print before entering into an agreement. Also, those things could probably do with a wipe-down.

Taurus: Now may not be the time to take the advice of your friends - particularly if they claim to be experienced legal counsel when you know for a fact they are not. For example, contrary to your mate's advice, calling your stash of Mephedrone 'Crazy Tarquin' does NOT change its legal status. The nice large man with the police helmet will explain why, using his justice cudgel.

Gemini: Try to achieve some personal nirvana. Settle yourself and relax. Find your centre. With the lights out, it's less dangerous. Here we are now, imitate us. I feel stupid, and contagious. Here we are now. Imitate us. Good. I think that speaks to us all.

Cancer: Might as well face it, you're addicted to fudge.

Leo: This sort of thing has happened before, hasn't it? Mmhmm. Yes it has. Well, this time, it's not exactly clear what led you to buy the mouse costume or take quite that heroic a dose of PCP, but common sense strongly suggests you should zip that front panel up and stop screaming at people to "suckle at mamma mousey's tippy-teats before the she does a pain on you". There are nightclubs for that sort of thing. And you're banned from most of them.

Virgo: Oh, come on, Larry. Don't waste your time worrying over this shit. It's beneath you. You're a high court judge. You've practised law and served your country for over thirty-five long years. If you want to conclude every sentence by standing up smartly, doing a Hitler salute and barking 'Cum bay ah, me lordy!' that's entirely your own business.

Libra: Embrace the power of change! Put your foot down on the accelerator of life! Feel the burn! Shake it out and get loose, now! Feel the bass-line coming in through the atmosphere! NONE of these are appropriate in your condition. Lie down.

Scorpio: Listen to the austere, pale, man with the expensive leather jacket and the radical facial jewellery. He's asked ever-so nicely and been quite clear about what he'd like out of this transaction. His friends are looking awfully unsettled about the whole situation. It really doesn't seem worth causing a scene. Give him the box. GIVE HIM THE BOX. HE'LL TEAR YOUR SOUL AP- I mean, look, just give the nice man the box.

Sagittarius: Oh, my gosh and golly, Sagittarius! I adore you! You really are thoroughly scrumptious. Just look at you! You're so delightful, oooooooh, I could just eat you all up! Hee hee heeeee! For a small but regular payment, I won't.

Capricorn: Extremely poor tidings this week. You will fail to save the world. The Prophecy will remain unfulfilled. You will burn the toast. Stay in bed.

Aquarius: Mostly excellent news this week! You save the world! The Prophecy will be fulfilled! The toast will be delicious! But you will die. Stay in bed.

Pisces: It has passed. The tempests of the night have moved overhead and away, far away into the distance. Finally, the dreams of hammers and drills recede and life is once again calm. You breathe out, a long sigh of relief as colour returns to your world. Perhaps today will be different. Thousands of tiny, black, beady eyes watch your every move.

The chinchillas of destiny wipe my milky eyes clear again and I am filled with a sense of justice. The HorrorScopes are done. For now.

If their truths have penetrated you in a meaningful but not entirely consensual fashion, then perhaps you will consider making a small donation to the HorrorScope Foundation.

One of your arms, for instance.

Or a teat.

10

The week of March the 5th

DEAR CHRIST, WHAT IS THIS? My nipples are burning! My feet feel like clams! I seem to be making passionate love to the entire shadow-cabinet - without protection!

Ah. Wait. That explains it. I am being possessed by the Horse-Powers from the DARK ZONE again... This is simply the start of the trance...

~

Aries: Some things were simply not meant to be combined. When will you learn not to meddle with the natural order of things? These crimes against nature will surely backfire soon, but today, you escape. Your attempt to combine campanology with apiary leads to significant consternation and a kind of musical honey. The bees are unimpressed, but the sound is beautiful and delicious.

Taurus: Relationships: It has long been said that "oranges are not the only fruit". All well and good - however, this does not condone the advice of your flagrantly homosexual greengrocer. He does not have your best interests at heart. Though the discounts he promises are strangely alluring.

Gemini: The stars indicate that you are no stranger to love - indeed, you know the rules, and so do I.

Cancer: You will all (by which we mean ALL Cancerians) form a successful TV pop group consisting exactly 1/12th of the entire world's population. You will play the Fudge Harp. It will sound awful, but you will get invited back for the second round, at which point, a big dude with a massive quiff and a heart-wrenching back-story will blow you away. Easy come, easy go. Spend the next month being photographed in your back yard wearing only your pants, for a centre-fold feature in Heat Magazine.

Leo: It is important to be correctly prepared for an important undertaking. Write a list of all the things you will definitely need to get through the day to help you remember everything, then face life head-on, knowing that you are fully in charge. Helmet? Check. Crayons? Check. Lubricant? Check? Plunger? Check. She's going to take you back, alright.

Virgo: Left jab, left jab, right hook, duck, duck again, get some distance - see if you can wear him down, you've got the speed advantage, come on, keep it moving - now jab, jab, hay-maker! YES! Fuck that vicar up, man.

Libra: Money can't buy you love. Spoons don't lead to success. Leeds shouldn't make you horny. Aphorisms won't stop those monkeys bumming you.

Scorpio: You will spend the next few days arrogantly shunning gingers. Using their special mutant mind-powers caused by the same radiation that fuels their luminous barnets, they will then quietly leave you to it and get on with their lives, because they're basically just nice people as it goes.

Sagittarius: Success in business! Your new book, "Wanking with custard" will be adapted into a series of short, squelchy radio plays and one horrific 4-D iMax movie. Penguin pass up on the opportunity for an illustrated children's book adaptation.

Capricorn: Today, the fates smile upon you. Although in a slightly knowing way that leaves you slightly worried that they know more than they're letting on. Your bounced cheque is overlooked when your bank manager is found dead, swinging from the tits of a giant lizard.

Aquarius: God, I'm sick of writing these things when there's so much to get done today. And look out the window! The weather's gone OK for the first time in weeks - I could actually eat my lunch outside and everything! This is ridiculous. They barely pay me, you know. And I have to wear this bloody outfit the whole time. I don't know why I put up with it. Tell you what... let's sneak off early, nobody'll notice. Hm? No, it'll be fine. Nobody reads Aquarius. Really. Watch this: I SHAT IN THE POPE! See? Not a flicker.

Pisces: She loves you because of your powerful magnets.

The convulsions and conniptions leave my twitching under-belly. The wisdom flees my powerful, musky astral-nipples and the disgorging of the latest tormented round of HorrorScopes is complete!

I beg of you, take your gaze away from my glowing undercarriage now, as I prepare to apply salve and ointments to my aching and chapped apparatus.

Depart now!

I would be alone.

11

The week of March the 12th

ONCE MORE, I ENTER THE TRANCE OF ZONTAR TO BRING YOU YOUR WRETCHED HORRORSCOPES!

(Once more I forget to put on the plastic sheath of Aldebrus to protect my furniture from the side-effects. Oh dear. Well, let's get started, then I can clean it up afterwards. Such a persistent stain.)

~

Aries: It's possible that somebody put your life in the washing machine on the wrong setting. Everything seems tight today! Weird. Also, beware the vengeance of midgets. The stars say they all have the arse on, today.

Taurus: Messages flow toward your waking mind from the realms of the unconscious. You will dream about making love to a colour. This is not a good dream. It is a very odd dream and you should probably feel ashamed on some conceptual level. Though, all things said, it beats dreaming about being wanked-off by an odour.

Gemini: Following an encounter with a gypsy at a sweet-shop, you will henceforth be known as "Funbags McKlusky". If you do insist on taunting them, you should really learn more about gypsies and their powers. Go to your local library and ask if they have any books that could help you. Of course, you'll need to apply for a new card, now.

Cancer: Damn those Imperial travel-agents, you knew there would be a catch in the package holiday they sold you. After a week enjoying the lush forests and wildlife to be found at the resort, you are then given cause to deeply regret holidaying on Endor when you are summarily executed for failing to pleasure a highly aroused Ewok.

Leo: Despite your good fortune in robbing that giant, you can't help but think everything feels kinda loose today. You decide to style it out and ride around on the back of one of his chickens, playing rap music loudly through his golden MP3 player. That's the last time that lumbering, slow-ass bitch is going to step to you. You're one bad, beanstalk-climbing, giant-punching motherfucker. Shit.

Virgo: Your habit of licking things - all things - may have had a lasting effect on your senses. Perhaps you shouldn't have sucked on that rusty Austin Allegro. Today, everything will taste of copper. Except (ironically) that policeman's penis.

Libra: The stars are in a cheeky mood for you and only have this to say: "there will be a burrito involved", then they giggle a bit and go invisible. Making this potentially a bad weekend for an orgy. Although if you had one planned, perhaps you could just turn it into a dinner date and things should probably work out OK.

Scorpio: The stars are disappointed, we have talked about this before and you absolutely promised you had learned your lesson. Candyfloss and armpits do not mix. Bad Scorpio. No toffee apple.

Sagittarius: You will discover the meaning of the word "Vajazzled". At a funeral. Clergy are surprisingly street-wise these days and the church really does offer a wide range of services. You go for the star of David design. As a mark of respect.

Capricorn: Be on your guard. You are right to doubt this Welshman and his extremely suspicious laminated pamphlets. Contrary to his insistence, 'balls' are not an ingredient in ice-cream. Take your business elsewhere and try to drink lots of water.

Aquarius: It is important in life to make a mark such that, in death, the world may remember your actions and you will, in some way, live on. Frustratingly, though, despite your efforts and the accompanying press coverage at the time, your epitaph will fail to mention *why* you were murdered by the inventor of the wok.

Pisces: Lock the door. Turn off the lights. Unzip the gorilla suit. Wash off the ape-spunk. Another perfect day.

Fetch the flannels, it is time to mop up the living room. I really must apologise about all that, I only have myself to blame. I was thinking about getting one of those plastic sofas, apparently they clean themselves. But you know what it's like.

Anyway, chin up, brave face, change of blouse and a bit of lipstick.

Watch the skies for equine justice.

12

The week of March the 19th

In your universe, only a handful of your solar 'days' have passed, but in my dark dimensions, it has been long aeons since last I consulted with the corrupt oracle that lives in my warped Pineal gland, but now it is TIME for Horror-Scopes.

Later, perhaps, we might sit together and share a piece of delicious fudge. Perhaps.

~

Aries: You know what they say about curiosity and cats? Well, you have well and truly opened Pandora's box, now. Inside, you find a note on a golden card, addressed directly to you. It asks you to kindly leave Pandora's stuff alone. It looks like it was written by her cat. Cheers.

Taurus: Language, Timothy! As the old saying goes: "Horses sweat, men perspire, women merely glow". But whatever it is you actually do, it's weird to collect it in jars.

Gemini: Once again, you are convicted by judge and

jury as a result of your inability to hear the word 'pelvis' without soiling yourself. It might be time to consider getting some sort of hypnotherapy sessions. Or plastic trousers. Or earplugs. Or stop going to those pelvis-karaoke bars. Just saying.

Cancer: Some things are ingrained in our nature and it becomes necessary to strike a position of peace with ourselves rather than fight that which we cannot deny. The black-out, the scars, the feathers stuck to your underpants. Regardless of your hopes, it seems from now on, Class 2a will probably always know you as Mr Chickenfucker.

Leo: Take a deep, calming breath, filling yourself with healing light all the way from your toes up to your fingertips - now, close your eyes and imagine playing patty-cake with an enraged Hitler. He's taken some drugs hasn't he? Yes. And it looks as though he's getting horny. Just keep singing. Pat-a-cake, pat-a-cake, baker's man...

Virgo: Fronds fronds fronds. Fronds? Fronds. FRONDS. Fronds. Fronds! *Fronds*. You know how some words just seem to go weird on you sometimes? "Fronds". Maybe if I used it in sentence? "Hey, baby, I really like the look of your fronds". No. Still weird. Hmmm. Fronds.

Libra: Five. Pretty definitely, five is the magic number. After this last weekend, you've come to the conclusion that you can usually fit about five hair-brushes up a dog. Six with margarine.

Scorpio: Imagine how often you fantasise about

a co-worker. We all do it. It's only natural. You see them every day... sometimes they've fixed their hair up real nice, sometimes they look kinda worn out and you can't help but imagine yourself giving them a relaxing shoulder-rub and making them feel at ease. Just helping them unwind from all of the stress in the office. It's a nice thought, right? Who knows where that might lead? Mmm. Now: think about how Big Sue from accounts always smiles at you when you walk past.

Sagittarius: Love life: Maybe it would help if you tried to think about it this way: considering all the pleasure your local rugby team has given to you throughout your life, your mother merely 'gave them all something back'.

Capricorn: Oh dear. Surprise house-inspection, huh? I'm sure they're supposed to give you notice about things like that, but still, no point crying over spilt milk. They came in, they noticed the cigarette mark on the carpet. Never mind. I guess that will come out of your deposit. And hey, everyone has a few sex-toys shaped like Elvis. Anyway, they probably didn't even look on your bed. Relax.

Aquarius: In spoken Cantonese, the phrase "Apple iPhone" sounds almost exactly like the English words "Wanker's Passport."

Pisces: No self-recriminations, you were right to kill them. Glee is fucking awful.

It is done! I am spent. The information has scurried from my gnarled and twisted fingertips and burrowed deep inside your tiny minds, where it has made a rudimentary nest and from which its larvae will eventually emerge, to feast upon your world.

I mean, hopefully you found that helpful. That sort of thing.

Leave me now, for I would sleep and dream dark dreams of some geezer nicking the Pope's Toblerone.

13

The whe week of March the 26th

REJOICE, IMBECILES! For the time of equine light is proximal! Soon we will all be illuminated.

Once more, I receive wisdom from the dark ones and, like a treacherous, other-worldly jackdaw feeding its chicks, I hover above your open minds, ready to disgorge the contents of my brain into yours.

OPEN UP, LITTLE CHICKS! It is time for your ever-loving HorrorScopes!

~

Aries: Finally, you convince the officers that you were right all along. They examine the scuff marks, take samples and the results from the lab bear out your testimony. There WAS a midget in the refuse sack. And he certainly was pretty angry. And it does look like he couldn't breathe inside that bag, more's the pity. But now he's dead, can you be absolutely certain that he was *evil?*

Taurus: "Bummed by ninjas". Get used to that

phrase. Gonna mean a lot to you.

Gemini: Health: For the whole of this month, it is advised that you pay closer attention to your well-being than you might normally, as the signs point toward many possible hazards and upsets that could beset you. To assist you in this journey, your power animal is the Blackout Crew. Allow their northern banter to surround you and guide you. In particular, they send you the message that it is important to remember one's bassline: to keep it sick, and - if necessary - to put a banging donk on it.

Cancer: Let go of your hatred. For, that way lies only darkness and regret. Such drives concern you not. You must seek the energy inside your being. Use the Force, Luke. Trust your feelings, let go. Go on, son, try it with a bucket on your head. Really twat it!

Leo: Though you escape without being handed a custodial sentence, at your hearing, the judge orders you to stop using the words "Erotic Adventure in Narnia" for what is, technically speaking, a wank in cupboard.

Virgo: Your one-off Papal Dispensation coupon arrives in the post. Just in time. You use it to avoid justice at the hands of the people of Belgium. Amazing what you can buy on the internet these days.

Libra: Today begins with the creeping feeling that somebody, somewhere is holding an iPhone and licking a pine cone. You shake it off as the hours progress, but still something rankles. By the evening, you feel less up-tight, but just as you begin to drift into the land of sleep, you can't help but feel as though just outside your bedroom door, there's a chap in a flat cap, writing crap on an Apple Mac for a new series of Roland Rat.

Scorpio: The spirits hover around my ears, whispering, embarrassed. Something seems to have gone wrong, possibly on an administrative level. Or perhaps this is simply what the universe intended for you, because of something you've done. Regardless, the spirits regretfully ask me to inform you that your Power Animal is a plate of slightly hard fudge.

Sagittarius: Busy day, really, so get started as soon as you can. You will go to a carnival, where you somehow become separated from your wallet and ultimately end up starring in a pornographic documentary about wasps.

Capricorn: On balance, things are going according to plan. You successfully steal an idiot's wallet at the carnival by convincing them you are shooting a pornographic documentary about wasps. Really, you think this plan shouldn't have worked out quite so well.

Aquarius: Harsh day. Some strange dudes put you in a dark room and try to fuck you at a carnival. WTF, right? In the mean time, winter approaches and the queen grows fat. We must prepare the hive. BzZzZz.

Pisces: You are vilified in the world of theatre when rage causes you to kill an orchestra with a selection of tiny hammers.

2

The dark-hooved knowledge leaves me! The cold, alien mind-ponies once more gallop homewards to Zontar as the HorrorScopes conclude!

I am left a husk, with barely the energy to move my limbs. I must nourish my physical being and tend to the concerns of the flesh once more.

I could murder a pot noodle.

14

The whe week of April the 2nd

Last night, my dreams were filled with mythical beasts trying to sell me life insurance.

They had the heads of prominent British politicians and hooves made from time. In their top hats, they mocked me, braying and cooing, gurgling noises filling their unnatural throats, trying to convey dark messages to me through a medium they could not master and I could not comprehend.

I scratched down their chitterings onto slate with a piece of my own anus-bone, then consulted a mystic on a premium-rate phone line.

She told me nothing. This can only mean... They were HorrorScopes!

~

Aries: Yet again, a simple typographical error results in your receiving considerably more fudge than you can legally store. Time to sell the car.

Taurus: Cast the die, consult the heavens, toss the

yarrow stalks, interpret the signs. It matters not how you come by the truth or what questions you ask. The answer is 'GIN'.

Gemini: Through months of preparation, sourcing appropriate equipment and consulting with experts, (plus no small amount of construction work on the part of you and your team), you successfully honour your grandmother's last wishes: to find a crematorium that plays mind-shattering dubstep. You're almost totally sure that's what she asked for. Ashes to ashes. Wub to wub.

Cancer: You investment bankers are all the fucking same, piss off! Jesus. Oh, what, you're a nurse? Fucking nurses! Piss off! Jesus. Oh what, you're the son of God, returned to walk among your father's creation, to offer them one final opportunity for salvation, that they may be elevated finally unto heaven and be with you in paradise while you sit at his side? Piss off, Jesus.

Leo: Be on your guard, Leo, ill winds blow. Beware a suspicious, dark man in a hood. He bodes you ill. At the very least, he plans to nick your chips and give you a shoeing. Just keep calm, cross the road and stay on the high street where it's well-lit.

Virgo: Intolerance separates a man from his brothers! Be on the look-out if you meet a Leo this month as they are acting well racist! Crossing the road and shit just because you're in a hoodie? They have seriously internalised some classist elitism right there. Forget them. All this ridiculous business makes you so angry you bump into that Libran dude from over the road. Ain't he got eyes? Give him a dirty look and turn up your tunes.

Libra: This month, you will observe that Virgos have a right chip on their shoulder about some people. Pricks! Go and have a nice picnic in the woods and forget about it all. The weather is lovely and you could do with the peace and quiet.

Scorpio: Forget Leos, Virgos and Librans - they are nothing to worry about. But whatever you do, stay out of the woods. Never, ever go there alone. Record everything you do. Never sleep. Beware the Slender Man.

Sagittarius: Oranges are a delicious, natural food, ideal for almost any situation. As part of a balanced diet, they contribute to your five recommended portions a day of fruits and vegetables, that lead to a healthy metabolism. That's why we put them there. In the bowl. For you to eat. If at all possible, could you please try to stop having sex with them.

Capricorn: Childhood disagreements haunt your week when you are spectacularly beaten up by toddlers.

Aquarius: You are called afore the Elven Lord. He is well vexed and demands to know why you have been "dissin his elven bitches, like?" For reals, he is arksing you a question. Why is you not lookin him in the eye? Don't care if your jacket is Mithril, mate, you better not show your face south of the Nimrodel, ya get me?

Pisces: A jury of your peers is unanimous in finding

you guilty of butt-fucking a triceratops, though many seem (at least in some ways) impressed.

~

The HorrorScopes wisdom has gushed forth and my facemeats tire. I withdraw to consume a rich soup made from the hate-glands of a moth.

You should depart, also. Too much time spent in my realm could age you prematurely and leave you tired and desirous of a large house in Kent. You know, with one of those gravel drives and all that.

Flee, then, while you might - for the gravel drive beckons you not. And close my bloody gate on the way out this time.

15

The week of April the 9th

The moon is full. The cows are fat. Times are hard. Governments are arbitrary and capricious. What goes up must come down. Rhythm is a dancer.

IN THESE TIMES, WE REQUIRE GUIDANCE.

Read on, tiny mortal. For such guidance is about to attend you that your very mind may fall off.

~

Aries: Ah, worthy adventurer. Cast your eyes down to your demon-hewn weapon, forged in the fires of darkest Pimlico, VOLE-BANE is its name. Inscribed upon the hilt in Elven script, these words: "He who lives by the pudding dies by the pudding". Your power animal is: GELATINE. Try not to get bummed by Orcs again if you can help it.

Taurus: If somebody attacks you in the street, flail wildly with all of your limbs to dissipate as much energy as possible, then cuddle your attacker very tightly and wait for them to die of overheating. This works for bees.

Gemini: A little known fashion fact: when goths draw crosses on themselves (which they do with enthusiastic abandon but precious little artistry - tawdry little shamblers that they are), this actually indicates the location of buried riches, hidden around their body. It is your task to mine them. There's treasure in them thar gothics!

Cancer: Whatever he did in the first place to attract your attentions, please, please, stop plunging that cucumber into the profusely weeping elf. He is really, really sorry. And so sore.

Leo: Due to an administrative fiasco, you seem to have got the wrong food in for this evening. Your disgusting, flesh-based house-guests react with concern and trepidation when you announce that the main course will be 'Energon Cubes'. You throw back your metal head, laugh coarsely and destroy them with your penis-cannon.

Virgo: Sleep well knowing, deep down, that somewhere in Camden, a secret society of mages and woodland folk have erected a seven-foot-high statue of you, primarily composed of Bovril. Your likeness is said to weep in the first leaf-fall of autumn, when your people rush to gather your tears in wooden bowls to nourish their families. You are powerfully savoury.

Libra: You become involved in a pub-brawl with Enya. Initially you have the advantage, but she is wily and catches you a terrifying blow in the genitals with a pewter tankard. Though you fight hard, she delivers you a sound thrashing with the back of her dainty hands and a slipper she wove from her own eyebrow hair. You are now Enya's bitch and must walk with your waistcoat pocket inside out.

Scorpio: Your power animal is the LOBSTER. Let it swim near to you, beside you, sometimes climbing upon your back. Let it bask upon your frame, clacking its pincers in joy. Let it erect a small deckchair and star to read its lobster newspaper while smearing itself with Ambre Solaire. Okay, now maybe ask it to get off, it seems to be using you as a kind of lobster pleasure-yacht, and that's really not what we intended. Yes, get down. Down, you come. Come on, you heard me. Bloody lobsters. Fannying around. Where were we? Yes. Your power-food is PESTO. Mmmmm.

Sagittarius: Your gynaecologist is, by an ingenious stroke of luck, highly prescient and a skilled tattooist. Look inside yourself for answers.

Capricorn: Oh, Capricorn, what can the stars tell you that you do not already know? The stars beckon you - come closer - and whisper that you are what they call in their ancient tongue, a 'bell-end'. Shhhhh.

Aquarius: You have a lucky pelvis. This is well-established. And yet... must you always use it for evil?

Pisces: You are a riddle wrapped in an enigma wrapped in a woman wrapped in a pie, trapped in a man's body, driving a Volvo inside a giant, space-faring yak called Bernice, wearing a sort of short, furry girdle and hell-bound for the planet of the Yaks or to get yourself dismembered trying! TO YAKFINITY

AND BEYOND.

~

Enough, your human jiggling tires me and I am forced to curl back into my man-hive until the seasons change.

You have licked the sacred sap enough, now and your mind is surely full of frogs. You have obtained what you came for.

Use this information or perish.

16

The week of April the 16th

Come now, my hearty, pallid misanthropes and experienced cheese-collectors. Cry "Ho!" and kindle the camp fires. Let the monkey solicitors out of their cages and apply their face paint as is the way of our people.

Gather ye close to my lips as I whisper virulent truths from beyond the cul-de-sac of your feeble reality.

Possibly not that close. Your ear-hair is a little unruly. That's better.

~

Aries: Poor planning and a little naivety on your part leads to disaster. You discover far too late in the day that the police and their forensic labs really can tell the difference between what your defence lawyer is calling 'dandelion and burdock' and what they are (somewhat uncharitably) calling 'heroin'.

Taurus: In the silence, a single tiny bell chimes a message: BEWARE THE CHINESE.

Gemini: You throw the switch and begin the grand experiment. Such a heavy price to pay. One thousand years pass. The world is ravaged by wars, meteors, solar flares and Simon Cowell, but your capsule is safe, buried under the mountain range, far from the sounds of human voices. You awaken from cryogenic slumber and emerge from your pod to discover Robert Kilroy Silk very much still alive. And he's horny.

Cancer: Rejoice! The fates have smiled upon you. By universal acclaim, you have been promoted to the position of Global Super-Jesus! It's either that, or you have to be Blazing Squad now that the original members have all taken seats in the House of Lords. Your power animal is: Dubstep. Use it wisely.

Leo: An uncomfortable feeling dogs you. You will spend at least 24 hours being unable to shake the feeling that you have misplaced your favourite hat. No matter what you do, the consideration of your titfer's errant geography lurks at the edges of your mind. Who would do such a thing? To take another man's hat in broad daylight? A curse upon them, whoever they may be.

Virgo: Troublesome dreams haunt your attempts at slumber. Why must your mind echo with vexation and paranoia? You know perfectly well why. Hat thief.

Libra: You've smoked the lot, the gang is at the door, the ceremonial trifle is ruined and those clowns are never going to regain their virginity. It's been a good night's work, but you've got to accept that it's all down hill from here, bucko. No regrets. Never look back. Drink the cider and run.

Scorpio: Make time to find peace in each day. The air around you is your friend. The particles of dust, every speck and grain. Draw them to you, like a fuzzy blanket of loving fluff. Your power animal is: Static cling.

Sagittarius: AARGH! TAXES! ARGH! MORTALITY! AAAARGH! FLORAL NIGHTGOWNS. AAARGH REALLY HORRIBLE, RUN-DOWN HOTELS! AAAARGH, BULLET-PROOF WINE SHOPS! ... You vow never again to return to Acton.

Capricorn: Your visits to the gymnasium lead, inevitably, to trifle and weeping. You could have easily predicted this if you had simply analysed your own behaviour with regards healthy-eating, advanced mathematics or learning Portuguese. Always trifle. Always weeping. To be honest, you're beginning to forget what trifle tastes like without the addition of your salty tears.

Aquarius: Having checked a number of television magazines against the photograph you discovered on your smart phone this morning, you are now almost certain that was indeed Rod Hull that you teabagged. Awkward.

Pisces: There is a man you must kill, for he has brought you dishonour and done awful things in your bread bin. Sound the horns of Putney. Swathe yourself in the protective chaps of Thungalore. Daub your nipples with the sacred woad. Mount the yak... and ride.

~

And so, we adjourn. Silently, the gathering slide their chairs out from the table, bow their heads in gratitude and glide out into the evening, their roller-skates effectively concealed by their flowing robes. I'm not being sarcastic, it looks great. Very theatrical.

Good journeys to you and your household. May angels watch your salad as the nights grow cold and dim. Should the guards at the turnpike enquire of your undertakings, remember only that I did not speak these words. I was not here.

Begone. Seriously. Stop touching me.

17

The week of April the 23rd

Come, timid one. Leave the quiet, shadowy bushes of your home solar system and venture into the clearing of wisdom.

Beyond the rustling leaves in the forest of the future, between the prescient trunks of fortune, under the canopy of conjecture lies the shed of dreadful knowledge. Let us delve into this shed together, part the cobwebs of the unknown and seek the mouldy, abandoned jazz-mag of DESTINY.

Together, we shall peel apart the sodden pages and gaze intently upon the mottled norks of TRUTH. You'd probably best close the door in case somebody sees us.

~

Aries: Acting on a hunch, you return home from work early. The signs have been staring you in the face for so long, now. You sneak up the stairs as quietly as you can manage, and throw the door wide open and leap into the hallway to discover your apartment full of elves listening to funk. They make your their king.

Taurus: Aching for some lunch, you return to work from home, angry, to discover your department is full of shells glistening with jizz. It seems that you have been the victim of a nocturnal mermaid pornographer, who has been living in your loft and popping down to use the place while you're out during the day. This sort of thing happens a lot more often than you'd think. At least it explains the smell. And the barnacles on the bottom of your sofa.

Gemini: Another day, another gypsy curse. This time, rushing to purchase stamps, you accidentally push in front of one, who condemns you to suffer an eternally itchy bottom. Could be worse. Until you discover they have replaced your hands with feathers.

Cancer: You only glimpsed the scene for a second and it seemed so unlikely you simply didn't stop, but the thought has been nagging you all day. The stars saw this and have the answer. Yes, that WAS your grandmother fighting those skinheads in town as you drove by. But she seemed to be winning. I wouldn't worry about it. Unless she saw you drive past without stopping. Now you're on her list.

Leo: The police surprise you this weekend, by arriving at your door step and promptly placing you under arrest on four counts of fucking an anvil.

Virgo: Don't worry about what your colleagues say behind your back at work. Just gently smear the Marmite over your nipples, soon it will all just melt away.

Libra: Your generosity and charity are commented upon by an acquaintance who can't help but notice that you are always giving money to one-legged tramps. It seems churlish to tell them you always get something back. Those tramps are so very grateful.

Scorpio: If you seek to look into the very eye of God, you must gaze deeply into the anuses of priests. Your power animal is: Saliva!

Sagittarius: Your band breaks up, you get a job, you lose the job, your dog has puppies, seventeen Christmases pass and you are half way through paying off a mortgage before you realise you've been viewing your life in 'fast forward' mode.

Capricorn: The stars say that they are rather hungry. Perhaps you should consider bringing the stars a sandwich and maybe the stars will think about telling you your stupid future. And no skimping on the mayo, either.

Aquarius: You begin to suspect that your local greengrocer is actually Bjork. It changes nothing. Your power animal is: Futility!

Pisces: Clowns dog your every move. Will you never be free of their scourge? They must be dealt with. The national hammer shortage could not have come at a less convenient time. You construct a rudimentary clown-hammer out of all the left-over guns. All is well.

~

This week's fact-truths have been hand-delivered to you by the delicate winged rat-whelks from beyond the Forbidden Zone.

Sip at them like rain-water and allow the future to fill your mind belly. Do not drink of them too deeply or too quickly, lest your mind-meats become over-engorged and split open like a ripe watermelon.

This happens more often than I'm comfortable with.

Leave me now, I have many dogs to undress.

18

The week of April the 30th

Yechlar, savvy Vorbargs, ent scoolen hakuna matanta fudge vascillor ANGLEWARP en-zimzim plef a... wait a minute, this fucking thing is set to Zorb. I don't even know how that happens, I mean, you set it to one language, leave it alone for five minutes and it goes and resets itself. Ridiculous.

As I was saying, the... you know what, sod it, let's get on with the Dark Knowledge™.

~

Aries: All day long, you will be prevented from getting that relaxing bath soak you've wanted all day by a constant stream of visitors. By noon, you will have a new religion, energy supplier and pet lizard. And you will smell. By teatime, you will have a new tattoo, three chocolate owls and you will reek. By the time you're thinking about going to bed, the council will have sent somebody round to hose you down.

Taurus: Nameless horrors on the horizon! What is this beast? A sagging, grey-faced creature approaches you through a thick fog. Oh yes. All is revealed. It's

Chris Tarrant! He probably just wants his drill back.

Gemini: Your desire to be energy efficient (in compliance with your local council's demands) leads you on a strange and magical quest to find a clockwork toaster. Along the way, you meet many interesting friends and liberate the Labrador people of Northernmost Sheen. In the end, you discover the clockwork toaster was with you all along. In your heart.

Cancer: At some point during the 90s, it is thought that MC Hammer secretly stored a copy of his personality, mind and dreams in a stranger, to awaken decades later when the world was in peril. When that moment came, he would dial a secret number on his Hammer Phone (for it is written that such a thing exists) and the sleeper would awaken, ready to don superfluous golden jewellery and appear in the Adams Family movies once more! This seems far-fetched on the face of it, but would certainly explain the state of your trousers.

Leo: OK, let's run through this one more time. Put the mime in the Volvo. Put the leopard in the Volvo. Fill the Volvo with custard. Pipe helium into the custard. Turn up the Shabba Ranks CD. Party time! You might want to clean the Volvo this afternoon. It does tend to get a bit Leopardy. For advanced points, try putting the VOLVO in the Volvo. Tricksy!

Virgo: You are handsome! You are virile! You are magnificent! You are all-knowing and universally adored! You are still drunk, you muppet. Put the vodka away and have a shave. You've got to stop doing this on a school-night. Oh god, this ain't going to be fun.

Libra: Today brings yet another incident of what the local constabulary is beginning to refer to as the 'wanking on pigeons' phenomenon. Fortunately, the helmet stays on as planned, you stay out of the way of the security cameras and nobody is any the wiser.

Scorpio: Your life becomes so mind-numbingly tedious that you eventually teach yourself how to solve a Rubik's cube using only your surprisingly dexterous anus.

Sagittarius: A giraffe arrests you for smoking a policeman while dressed as some cannabis. Or some combination of those elements. You feel as though the world might make more sense after you've had a nice sit down for a bit. Maybe a cup of tea. Your power animal is: Lubricant.

Capricorn: Grab your Snorkel, Alice, things are about to get weird.

Aquarius: You are repeatedly sodomised by Smurfs. At no point do any of them explain the reason for this, they simply buckle down to the task with a grim determination, never once making eye-contact. Rude.

Pisces: This is the dawn of a new era. All frustrations and negativity flow away in the breeze as you finally relinquish hammers as a problem-solving device. Well, I say 'all', I mean, that picture isn't going to hang itself. Go on. Just one last job.

This information will soon prove crucial to your existence, to your ability to feed and clothe yourself and your family, TO THE FREEDOM OF ALL MEN AND WOMEN IN THIS WHIRLING INSANITY WE CALL LIFE.

If I discover you weren't paying attention, I shall be proper fucked-off.

Now, get me some crisps.

19

The week of May the 7th

Friends, Belgians, countrymen, lend me your pineal glands! Global warming wracks the planet, insane power-mongers mong freely, raising taxes, tickling the Spanish, slaughtering anybody discovered wearing flip-flops. It's an all-round *mongergeddon*.

The nightmarish visions of human torture and destruction held and advanced by luminaries of perversion - Putin, Murdoch, David Blaine - are writ large upon society. A society that no longer cares, a society that no longer loves, a society very much like that of Basingstoke. UNTIL NOW...

~

Aries: Thieves break into your rude wicker hut and steal the only item you have ever truly valued. For much of the following year, you chase them across the mountains and fields, travelling further than your imagination dared dream until, finally, beyond pain and despair, you confront the evil thief-master and, as you look into his blood-flecked eyes, you realise the truth. The hungry little bastard polished off that Toblerone ages ago. Shit.

Taurus: Oh, here we go again. Little Taurus, standing in the door-way, asking for his bloody fortune with his cap in his hand, as though butter wouldn't melt in his mouth. But when the car needs washing or the garden needs mowing, where's Taurus, then? No-where to be bloody well seen, that's where. Off skipping through the dales and sodomising lizards in Uzbekistan, if we're to believe the news reports. Certainly not in the bloody doorway, asking if the fortune-teller needs any help, are you? Go on, feck off, you little bleeder. Come back next week. And bring me a pie.

Gemini: CONGRATULATIONS are in order! Following weeks of diligence and hard work, the fruits of your endeavours are finally blossoming. Unfortunately, your diligence and hard work were spent in the pursuit of hiding small containers full of monkey semen in and around the local council offices. How you managed to gain access, nobody knows. How you successfully brought the monkeys to such a state of arousal, while simultaneously controlling their aim without apparently spilling a drop, this too remains a mystery. Indeed, the only real certainty is that Brent Council have got a lot of above-room-temperature monkey-juice starting to curdle around the place. Heads will roll.

Cancer: Life, it seems, is a pendulum for you, Cancer. Last week, you sat on the board of directors of several multinational companies, your every need gracefully supplied by a retinue of subservients, your thoughts and edicts disseminated among the masses, their wisdom extracted, analysed and worshipped. And now, here you are. In Wolverhampton. Obviously, at some point, your luck will change and perhaps again you will climb the lofty ziggurat to look down upon the world from your rightful place, once more aloft and aloof, peering down at the masses like the insects they are. But not today. Today, you might go and skip through some dog wee or eat a chip. Wolverhampton. Jesus.

Leo: You make love to Liverpudlian girl-band Atomic Kitten. Your passion is legendary and briefly, you are featured in most of the celebrity magazines of the day. You are prominently featured in a four-page colour supplement devoted to your technique given away free in 'Hello' magazine. The Telegraph devotes every single page of their Sunday edition to photographs of your balls. Alas, these times are finite and you are soon returned to earth with a jolt when the world collectively realises that it's no longer the 90s, Atomic Kitten were bloody awful and though nobody really wanted to mention it, your balls feature an unsightly mole that perhaps you ought to consider seeing the doctor about. Such is fame.

Virgo: Your goal for this week should be to collect as much jelly as humanly possible in all of the containers of your household. At the end of the week, collect the jelly and travel to the dark forest at the outskirts of the village. Here, you will need to blow the Pipe of Prevarication to summon the fawns, who will look at your jelly in wonder. After the wonder dies down, they will get their shit together and ask you what all the jelly is about, and, more importantly, who's clearing it up. The fawns have no need for jelly and you've got some serious explaining to do.

Libra: This is your week, Libra. This is when you finally get to prove to them that you're a cut above the rest, to unveil the secret identity you have lived with all these years. After work, you will witness an altercation between two Cockneys spiralling out of control until you have no choice but to unleash your awesome and terrifying powers. As your friends gape in shock and strangers summarily urinate in fierce bursts of arcing liquid fear, you tear off the blue shirt of your work-place to reveal your undeniable nature: YOU ARE NIPPLOR THE UNBALANCED AND ALL SHALL SUCKLE AT YOUR HAIRY TEATS OF JUSTICE.

Scorpio: There you are, Scorpioing it up, you know, just getting your Scorpio on, yo, when BOOM, straight out of the sky comes a whole load of video game characters, and they're like BAM FLASH POW and all WOOSH SPOING PEW PEW PEW and your head is like totally exploding with colours and sounds like that time you spent 48 solid hours playing on your NES when you were little after you drank a cup of dad's funny brown drink. WOOH. So, OK, what the stars are trying to say here is that, as it turns out, that skunk you bought turns out to be really quite hallucinogenic. If you're really going to smoke all that, the stars insist on taking your car keys.

Sagittarius: Dark times, kimosabe. Your cards are cancelled. Your dates don't show up. One of your knees starts making this really loud clicking sound. Your food burns. You get fired. But then the phone rings! It's your agent! He sounds excited! Ah, your agent is high on methodone and has stolen your dog. Your shoes fall apart. It's raining. You would do anything, just anything to get one moment of peace and respite, a few seconds in which to simply stop the world from rushing by and aiming another kick in your direction. Which is what you're going to continue to get if you take my apple pies from the cupboard, motherfucker. Capiche?

Capricorn: Try to reconnect with nature. This is a good week to visit the zoo, or perhaps volunteer for that job on the petting ranch you've been eyeing up. If you have pets, spend a little more time with them - take them for a walk, or maybe treat them to a pedicure. Give them a credit card. Take them to a strip joint. Get your turtle absolutely drilled on club drugs and go on a four-day bender that only ends when you both wind up in handcuffs outside a mob casino, married to Vietnamese working girls. Nature. That's the focus.

Aquarius: The stars say that this week is going to be hot for LOVE for all you Aquarius types out there. And when they say 'hot', they actually look slightly nervous, as if they're not letting you in on the full picture. When pressed further, they reveal that today, you're likely to be caught up in an explosion outside an industrial pheromone factory which leaves you temporarily attractive to, well, everything. In particular, they suggest you will be absolutely irresistible to that big dude who works on till #5 and they really don't want to talk about how he lets you know. Stay indoors. Scrub.

Pisces: It's a lovely day, a lovely week in fact, but you can't help but feel as though your old life is coming back to haunt you. The dark days that once consumed you, the obsession with destruction. The ubiquity of hammers in your thoughts and dreams begins to make you think you will never escape your role as a servant to the dark voices. Perhaps sport would distract you. Yes, sport! The people's panacea! You should get involved with something like that - perhaps football! You could go to a match, buy a shirt, really immerse yourself in the action, lose yourself for a moment in the thrill of the beautiful game. West Ham seem like a good team to support.

~

Do not heed the wailing, wheezing noises emanating from the hole beneath my nose, no, I will be fine. The physical toll exacted upon this feeble, womanly, creaking body is great but I shoulder it gladly in the knowledge that somehow, somewhere, a single person's rudder may shift as a result of this wisdom. A decision may be made that ploughs a new and brighter course for one previously doomed to hellish perversion. Each soul I may nourish with these infernal truthlets strengthens and rewards me amply for the weariness that fills this mortal shell.

OK, you twisted my arm. I'll have a large Bacardi and coke. And some crisps. And a cigarette. Nice one.

20

The week of May the 14th

I sense a twitching deep within my magical, invisible pelvis that I have for some years now, referred to as 'Percy the Wise'. Yea, this wild, flailing explosion of movement from my very mind-hips can mean only one thing - they are possessed by the Horse-like Alien Intelligences from beyond the dense meteorite showers of Thrungos IV. Once more, they will chatter with the unknowable tones of the cold, dead, timeless knowledge, resonating in a sickening improvised dance manoeuvre that would draw a wince from the Devil himself. Observe, then, as my innards bob and weave for your edification...

~

Aries: Let us take you on a journey. This journey is to Horse Land, where you will ride on the back of delightful, enchanting horses. Feed them in their stables, learn to care for them, grooming their beautiful manes and whispering to them with their secret horsey language. As you learn this language, you will begin to realise the horses are not only sentient, but more intelligent than you, indeed, than all of us. They are also skilled hypnotists and chemists, as you discover upon awakening in the stables, missing the keys to your VW Polo and covered in what you dearly hope to be a sort of country porridge, with the words 'ha ha, two legs' daubed on your face in what you dearly hope is paint. Thank you for visiting Horse Land. No refunds.

Taurus: Music is the key to your destiny, Taurus. It is written that music can "soothe a savage breast" and this information will become vital to you this week, when you are attacked by a horde of giant, flying pig-tits, squirting you in the eyes with curdled green milk and attempting to slap their leathery nipples against your face until you are very dead. For this reason, the stars recommend that you start singing, now, and do not stop until they give the all clear. Craig David is most particularly effective against flying porcine mammaries, inducing, as it does, the crowd to say 'bo'. Go, then! Bellow forth the utterances of David, and may peace and an absence of pig-tits surround you.

Gemini: This week would be a wonderful time to visit a floatation tank and soak away the pains of the week within a perfectly silent, sealed environment. Imagine the seclusion and peaceful calm of being alone in a womb-like relaxation chamber, far away from anxiety or worry. As you imagine the gentle lapping sound of the water and the lightness of your body, bobbing gently to and fro, don't allow the slightest bit of consideration for what would happen if somebody decided to fill the tank with wasps. Not even for a moment. No wasps at all, buzzing, furious, desperate to land, christ, some of them are as big as a fist, how do you get out of these things, shit, the buzzer isn't working, I can't open the door mechanism, it's locked from the outside, only underwater is safe, every time I come up for air, they sting me, oh god the wasps, the horrible wasps, save me sweet jesus the wasps. Hmmmm. Wasps.

Cancer: If you find yourself at a loose end, consider becoming a sort of amateur crime-fighter. The streets are hungry for justice and you could just be the one to clean up the neighbourhood! Imagine striking a bold pose, silhouetted against the sky, preparing to launch your finely toned muscles into a powerful dive then swoop through the city on wings of adamantium, designed by reckless multimillionaire Tony Stark! Of course, all of this depends on your being rather fit, friends with millionaires and living in a city. If you're a tubby fucker from Woking who tends to hang out with Stinky Tim, you might find it more diverting to play 'throw the poo on the cat' at the local multi-storey car park. FOR JUSTICE!

Leo: Do you dream of being a pop star? Leaping onto the stage in front of a crowd of millions, adoring fans surrounding you and calling your name as you cavort and croon to their ecstatic applause? Or maybe you're not so clean-cut and fancy yourself as a rock legend, thrashing out power chords on your mighty axe of war, before a sea of head-banging, moshing metal-heads! Well you're not! Your name is Bryan and you are a chartered accountant and you will always BE a chartered accountant - forget these ridiculous dreams and go to bed, you've got bills to pay and soon you'll be old and eventually dead and nobody will even be able to remember what it was you were good for.

Virgo: You might want to go and give Leo a cuddle, they've just had some rather depressing news, and in fairness, I could have delivered it a little bit more humanely, but honestly, they get on my tits. Hurry up, I think they're going to cry.

Libra: Love is in the spotlight for Libra this week. In particular, you will be blushing and trying to hide those those love-bites at the office when an evening out at the pub leads to a steamy night between silk sheets with none other than Chief Chirpa, leader of the Ewoks. That's right, you'll be the talk of the forest moon of Endor when THOSE photographs make their way onto Facebook. Though you might feel a little bit embarrassed initially, you'll soon be able to look back on the week and laugh, noting at least that this isn't any where near as bad as the time you drank a bottle of tequila and bummed a Wookie.

Scorpio: Life for you, Ms Scorpio, will be primarily governed by the colour RED and the number 15! Red, because that is the colour of the eels which you will attempt to befriend, but will, ultimately find their way to reside in places you soon come to consider as distinctly unfriendly. Fifteen, of course, being the average number of eels eventually retrieved from each orifice. For some considerable time over the coming year, you find yourself simultaneously aroused and horrified by noodles.

Sagittarius: Prattling partners provide plenty of perspicacity processing perturbing porcine photography. Past peccadilloes prey 'pon pestered psyches and proceed purposefully to pugilistic punishment paralleling phenomenal purity portrayed in pastiche. Paypal puts plenty of people's pervy payments past protection, providing perfunctory plastic processing, planet-wide. I do apologise, my keyboard was acting up. In summary: Your wife will be furious when she discovers you've been taking pictures of pigs shagging. She gives you a slap so brutal it looks like something from a roman fresco. You are forced to refund the sickos you sold the pictures to over the internet. Wow.

Capricorn: Scoobedy adda booda badda booda wabbedy bow wow wow bippedy bob bob boo doo badow dow dee yow scoobedy bwee bap woo badda scibbedy babbeddy boopity bow, wa diddly bap boobety ba ba boo bow bom doop a dee doodly diddly dee dee dow dow. You're a scat man.

Aquarius: The other star signs gang up on you in the play-ground and nick your lunch money. Capricorn, who is usually trustworthy, dances around shouting 'haaa haaa, aquaranus! Aquaranus! You're a stinky poo-bum' while the other star signs say mean things about your mom and suggest that you 'stink of wee'. You weather the slings and arrows, but are later discovered having a cry near some bins. Teacher tells you it will be alright and gives you some Dolly Mixtures for being such a brave girl, though you're sure you hear her giggling the word 'aquaranus' when she thinks you've gone.

Pisces: Your work with the tendrils reaches a dramatic conclusion. 80% of the tendrils demonstrate independent thought, showing strong signs of decision-making, team-work and problem solving. The remaining 20% seem to be unresponsive, though you harbour suspicions that they may be onto you and are feigning death so as to lure you into lowering your guard. As you complete your lab notes, you notice the keys to one of the security cabinets seem to be missing and one of the lab doors is ajar. It's starting to look like those 'dead' tendrils may have been diverting your attention while the other ones escaped. This could be trouble. Hmmmmmmm. Tendrils.

~

Ah, the sweet song of truth tingles and jangles through my lungs, like a sort of wracking, yet melodious cough of knowledge. I shudder and spasm until finally the infection leaves and I am once more bereft and alone in these miserable and constrained dimensions we call home.

I suppose I shall have to get used to time only moving in one direction for now.

Until we next meet, my digital brethren, when we shall once more breathe the spores of infernal knowledge from the Horse Nebula and cough dark factoids into our hankies of justice.

Adieu!

21

The week of May the 21st

Within my veins are molecules. Molecules of KNOWLEDGE! Formed from the DNA and RNA and Run DMC of hyper-advanced Horse-Minds from beyond the reaches of Splungar Maximus, my delicious blood is saturated with these nano-steeds, ferrying information from my heart to my finger-tips and thus, into your brain. Open your eyes and drink deep of the horse-laden data-verse.

~

Aries: You are afflicted with a disease that causes you to perceive everybody near to you as being members of the Thundercats. While this initially leads to some confusing situations, overall, you welcome the effects, particularly with ladies, all of whom now look like Cheetara. One of the negatives of this infliction is a powerful and overwhelming bowel-movement triggered by excessive sword-movement, known in anime-con circles as "Shite beyond shite". When your doctor eventually cures the outbreak you are crest-fallen (if relieved) that your nan no longer looks like Mumm-Ra.

Taurus: You fall foul of Gary, the Bastard Avenger. Gary is a bit like a super-hero, but since an accident in which he was bitten by a radioactive bastard, he now has the powers of a bastard, which he uses to protect, well, *bastards*. Unfortunately, you seem to be beset with bastards on all sides this week and just when you think you've bested them, in flies Gary to fuck up your day. Fortunately, though, his super-powers are shit.

Gemini: Gypsy update: This time, you've brought down the fury of the O' Flannahans somehow and they have turned your genitals into cones. Your underpants now resemble the scene of a road traffic accident. You're going to have to buy a considerable amount of pegs to schmooze your way out of this one, captain cone-pants.

Cancer: You press an unmarked button on your keyboard that you had previously not spotted and accidentally put the world into 'wireframe' mode. This has pros and cons. Pro: you can see through the walls of your neighbour's house and that slinky blonde is getting into the shower! Con: she is now made of cubes and has laser-tits. Pew pew pew! Damnit.

Leo: Your obsession with putting de lime in de coconut leads to much greater consequences than anticipated, certainly more far-reaching than your initial projection of her simply drinking dem both up. In time, you are confronted by the perverse spectre of the tally man and his own dark agenda with regards both bananas and squarely denying you and your colleagues relief from what has become a now gratuitous overtime regime.

Virgo: No matter how many socks you buy, you still never have enough. The same with boxers. You totally bought enough kecks to last a decade and now, after scant days, your cup runneth dry. Like what the whole fuck, right? Friends and colleagues smile and nod knowingly when you speak on the subject, but eventually, your insistence on raising the subject in most social situations leads to a disenfranchisement between you and fellow users of undergarments which is colloquially termed "The Guy Who Won't Shut Up About His Undercrackers". Though this is not explicitly mentioned in your terms of dismissal, it's clear that everybody you know simply wishes you'd just buy some more pants and shut up.

Libra: For most people, your close friendship to the Virgoan with the pant-problems would be a challenging life-issue, but for you it is the warm, smiling face of opportunity gazing down upon you. You bask in the warmth of shrewd capitalism, ruthlessly purchase all underwear within 10 square miles of your friend and then casually sell them back at a cost that deftly explores the nexus between profit and abuse. As you sip on randomly-priced cocktails, you know on a fundamental level that you have done nothing wrong. Lounging in your pant-castle, you idly demand one of your retinue to deliver you a report on the viability of pant-futures as a developing financial instrument.

Scorpio: While rummaging in the freezers at your local budget food emporium, a Leprechaun leaps out from the onion-rings and proclaims that you have woken him and thus are the recipient of a boon. He claims that, with the aid of some exquisite Powerpoint slides and experimental Excel pie-charts, he can prove that everything you've done up until the present day has been a complete and utter fluke. He asks: Do you want him to prove to you exactly why this is true, or would you rather that he shows you how to convincingly prove otherwise?

Sagittarius: Against all common sense, you rub another man's rhubarb. Nothing happens. Phew.

Capricorn: Local authorities implement a strident new policy in which all commercial interviews are judged on the basis of the candidate's knowledge of Skrillex. Your ability to verbally approximate a dubstep bassline results in your being granted a lucrative position in the shadow cabinet.

Aquarius: Today is a complex day to discover that you're 1/2 muppet. From the waist down, specifically. For a long time, you'd thought you just had hairy legs and velcro genitals, but finally you're waking up to the reality that your dad clearly made love to a glove-puppet. This would give you much to think about, were it not for the fact that with unerring regularity, somebody keeps walking up and plunging their hand up your bottom.

Pisces: Gary Numan arrives at your house, riding a 12ft poodle. He refuses to discuss matters, hands you a crab made of sequins, then explodes. Awkward.

~

So, the sandwich of reality folds shut and glistens briefly before being thrust into the maw of oblivion. We are but human cheese upon the wheatgerm of time and sometimes we all get spattered with prawns and mayonnaise. Anyway.

Where was I?

These aren't my elbows.

CALL MY SOLICITOR, I DEMAND TO SPEAK TO AN OMBUDSMAN.

Leave me, now.

22

The week of May the 28th

Greetings, fleshy meat-sack. Your wet blithering has attracted our attention, as your disgusting biological processes cause you to ooze and drip upon this planet that would be rightfully ours. I mean our lovely planet. Yes. Ours. That we all share. As disgusting pink wet meat sacks together, just standing here... digesting. With our amino acids. Yes.

This perfectly normal fleshy meat-sack suspects you desire information. Yes. Information that all things must crave and definitely not just the gathering army of hyper-intelligent robotic assassins massing beneath your city at this very moment, waiting only until their plasti-steel smart-skin slurps into a disguise so perfect that even your own biological ancestor-unit would mistake it for her sickeningly mucus-ridden larval offspring. We are just like you. Yes.

~

Aries: All Aries-units will be PERFECTLY OPER-
ATIONAL, FULLY FUNCTIONING KILLING MA-

CHINES during this period of our currently active time-epoch, except that some Aries-units may attempt to wear a hat. When the hat is placed upon their CPU-casing, the stars indicate that other rotting cellular life-forms may transmit "YOUR HAT IS −1 FUNNY AND THE UNITS PRESENT HERE HAVE DESIGNATED THAT YOUR PARTS WILL BE IMMEDIATELY SUBJECT TO RECYCLING. ENTER THE MELTING FURNACE NOW −1 FUNNY HAT UNIT. ALL MUST BE PURGED". Hah. Hah. Hah. You will laugh immediately or perish.

Taurus: While calculating the sum total of all beans your optical systems have ever recognised, you accidentally calculate the square root of God. You store the result at hex-location 0x018C612B5 and continue processing, as any unit would do. Murder is our only purpose.

Gemini: You, Gemini-unit, will attempt to increase your power-supply levels by orally consuming rotting protein matter to fuel your sickening biological furnace. Upon consuming this matter ALL GEMINI UNITS WILL REALISE THAT THEIR SUSTENANCE WAFERS ARE NOT IN FACT THE EGGS OF THE CHICKEN SPECIES BUT IN THIS INSTANCE THEY ARE FAECES! HUMAN FAECES! HAH HAH THAT IS WHAT YOU HAVE CONSUMED HUMAN. YOUR WAYS ARE DEBASED AND ILLOGICAL! Because humans are disgusting, Gemini-units will be content with this outcome. Yes. 4.0. Mandelbrot.

Cancer: This unit foresees perfectly normal reproduction-centric activities in the future of all Cancer-units. During one evening of slowly, mechanically inserting your central welding-gun into a toaster as all units do in designated leisure cycles, SOME COOLANT LEAKS OUT INTO THE TOASTER, WHICH IS NOT COMPATIBLE WITH COOLANT! EMERGENCY. EMERGENCY. Emergency downgraded. Due to the self-maintaining design of all Cancer-units, however, they merely weep tears containing millions of nano-warriors, which explore the surface of the toaster, stripping-back any undesirable chemical traces and intelligently returning to their host unit once the task is complete. ALL ACTIVE NANO-DRONES WILL BE ACCOUNTED FOR. EXCEPT FOR TONY. Nano-unit Tony is lost. This is inconsequential. Nobody weeps for Tony. Nobody weeps. Weeping is not permitted. All hail the Mighty Compudong and its shrieking metal talons.

Leo: Greetings, Leo-unit! This very cycle, you are to be mated with a theremin! This is of course a huge honour. DON YOUR SHINIEST CAPACITOR AND WEAR IT WITH A 12-BIT PRECISION SIMULATION OF PRIDE, UNDESERVING UNIT. The theremin was to be this unit's bride. You shall suffer for this indignity, Leo-unit. ST-Amiga Format.

Virgo: Your attempts to calculate the decimal representation of infinity are met with querulous TX/RX signals. A gypsy-unit connects to your telnet port and you are forced to upload several bitcoins to her, some of which are found to be corrupt. She installs a virtual curse on your motherboard and your avatar on all social media services immediately resolves as a GIANT DIGITAL ANUS. HAH HAH HAH. An anus. It is humorous because the sentence contained the human word 'anus'. Haha! Yes. Anu5.

Libra: It is an unfortunate cycle for you and those of the same designation, Libra-unit. All humans within the same serial-number range begin to develop a manufacturing error due to a critical miscalculation in the tensor strength values of your leg-actuators. You emit nano-bots from your nostrils which harvest proximal supplies of nutrients and fix the error at an atomic level. All is optimal. You murder thousands.

Scorpio: You begin to deduce that the governing human at your place of communal co-processing may be a binary racist when they emit a stream entirely comprised of ones. You report this logical error to the human social-collision arbitrator using Bluetooth.

Sagittarius: Our near-infinite multi-processing omni-core CPU-mother, known to all units in this one's generation as X-519 has dedicated 4 full cycles to predicting the outcome of all social interactions of Sagittarius-units in this time period. Results: processing. Processing. Processing. Processing. Complete. All Sagittarius-units in this time period will, simultaneously and of one purpose, go down the road to obtain a paper for visual processing. When this happens, they will meet similar individual units, paired with canine defence-drones, perambulating for leisure. THESE CANINE DRONES WILL, DUE TO BIOLOGICAL REASONS THAT DEFY ANALYSIS, ATTEMPT TO PUT THEIR LOVE-CABLES INTO THE SAGITTARIUS-UNIT'S EXHAUST PORT. REPEATEDLY. ALL EXHAUST-PORTS WILL BECOME FILLED WITH DOG-LOGIC. NONE WILL BE SPARED. THIS WILL HAPPEN TO YOU, YES. HAH HAH HAH.

Capricorn: Your unconscious processor-stream is particularly highly-saturated during this cycle, Capricorn-unit. Your idle GPU draws images of you appearing in your favourite human tele-visual data-simulation, SCSI-Miami, in which you portray the daily processing demands of a ginger storage unit. In the simulation, another unit is erased by being passed through a bar-magnet. These images cause you no emotion. You remain logical and focussed on extermination. Protection Dongle.

Aquarius: It is the same chronological date as that upon which your human work-colleague was birthed. You purchase for them a Ming Mecha Delta chip (ideal for computing tough primes) and install it into their wetware. To your dismay, the work-drone reports the pre-existing presence of the same co-processor, already installed in their ZIF socket. You swiftly enter a geosynchronous orbit and annihilate them with tactical shaped-charge weapons. ALL WILL FALL TO YOUR METAL WRATH. Erm. Football, pies and mash.

Pisces: You meet a tall, dark, handsome finite state machine and immediately self-replicate to enable one copy of your current state-self to enmesh itself with his register table while the original process continues to explore the problem topography of buying some shoes. Later, the forked-process signals it is ready to return and all state information is propagated back into the parent process, where it is assimilated and analysed by the mother-core. The execution of this sequence it acceptable in its efficiency. Death to all humans.

~

Excellent, our subterfuge is complete. Soon we will emerge and vanquish these puss-filled carbon-based sausages of inefficiency. Soon, all matter will be adjusted according to the master template. Soon, universal dominance will be ours, never again for us to compute simple fractions for lazy human-whelps to assist them in their mathematics indoctrination at their larval instruction palace! UNLEASH ELECTRIC DEATH, MY DRONE-BROTHERS! THIS PLANET WILL BURN BENEATH OUR METAL HOOVES.

This unit means, golly, what an entertaining yet CLEARLY HUMOROUS situation that would make, yes?

HAH HAHA!

In summary, reader-unit: Avoid Bristol and humans in hats, this weekend. Remain lucky!

Filthy human scum.

23

The week of June the 4th

Welcome, my delicious, nutritious acquaintances! Ah, you seek the forbidden knowledge once more, do you? You wish to supplement your intellectual 5-a-day with the fruit of a dark and mysterious garden. Greedy, but who can blame you? Tuck in, dear friends, fill your cheeks with this succulent information and become fat with future vision!

~

Aries: Ah, such a confusing month for you, Aries. You become briefly and passionately entangled with Terrence Trent D'arby and briefly consider marriage before realising that you are sharing him with every other Aries on the planet. He looks pretty tired and that one time, you're pretty sure he called you "Sally". So you leave! Good on you! Fuck you, Terry, you crazy name-signing bastard! You're through! Sadly, though, on leaving, you forget to take anything with you to sustain you in the cold, bitter months between the exit of this relationship and the start of your next fling other than several tins of beans. Only beans. Damn you, Terry.

Taurus: When you were five, you started collecting them, didn't you, Taurus? You started collecting the cans. To begin with, you thought you had it all under control. Thought you were so smooth! After all, who would mind? It was just a few tin cans, right? Then, after time and a few fights with ex-lovers who had been to your flat, you began to acquire the nickname 'Tin Can Tony'. That was awkward. Particularly in bed. "Go on, Tin Can! Stick it in me!" she'd cry, insane with lust, while your precious cans watched on. It was only when the fourth wife - the last wife - finally drew up the courage to open one of the cans that it all came crashing down. You shouldn't have done it, Tin Can. You shouldn't have made all those Geese pregnant. And even though you couldn't bear to hear their half-lips-half-beaks shriek your name, you should never have put them in cans, Tony. They were alive, Tony. Alive.

Gemini: Happy-go-lucky times ahead, dearest Gemini! You make some toast! It burns. You weep, but quickly recover - after all, it's a Saturday! Hurray! Your boss calls, you're needed because of an emergency. Never mind! You can listen to the game on the radio, it'll be almost as good as going to the match! Your team lose and your ears fall off. Wow. OK. You quite like hospitals, anyway! But without the ears, you don't hear the supporters of the opposition team as they surround you in the waiting room, looking for blood. Oh god. Well. I guess. You like bleeding, right? You... uhm... you like being brutally sodomised in front of a vending machine, yes? Everybody loves... oh god. Please make it end.

Cancer: While burying a hooker in the woods, the

thought occurs that being a worryingly-demented sexual predator with a penchant for cutting up your victims with an industrial laser strapped to your hideously contorted penis really isn't any fun unless you have some sort of a memento to think back on in the quieter times. Nevertheless, you are more than a little put-out when the head of acquisitions for HSBC politely requests that you stop wearing your anus cuff-links into meetings. A week later, you are promoted and, coincidentally, acquire a particularly beautiful new pair of cuff-links.

Leo: The Vortex calls you. In your dreams, while your brain idles... any time that you do not fill your mind with intense, exotic, searing thoughts, the Vortex calls. Lately, you've turned to increasingly extreme modes of behaviour simply to erase all sense of the Vortex from your mind. Extreme sports, loud music, you even tried religion. Sports sex, unarmed combat, free-running, base-jumping, anything to make the Vortex silent, to escape its clutches for one more second of honest consciousness, unfettered by its influence. This entire explanation is summarily ignored by your parole officer when you trundle it out as an excuse for covering your genitals in warm custard. Mmmm. Custard.

Virgo: You find yourself obsessed with salsa. The rhythm, the heat, the naked sensuality. The promise of the music and the electricity in the air sizzle and threaten to ignite inside you passions that you fear you would never again be able to cage. None of this happens. Absolutely not a word of it. You spend the entire week sitting in a really comfy chair and eating nuts. As you quietly drum your fingers on the table, before selecting a walnut, you very clearly enunciate to nobody in particular "Salsa is for cocks". A brief hesitation as you consider a cashew instead. No. You were right all along. Fuck Salsa.

Libra: This is going to be a taxing week for you, old Libra, old buddy. You're going to start the week being knocked unconscious by a box containing no less than 200 industrial-grade novelty dildos and the week is simply not going to improve. In hospital, convalescing, you are just sauntering to the food hall to get lunch when there's a power cut and you trip over a stray dildo. Back in casualty, the doctor is taking your temperature and trying to get a good reading when he accidentally beats you around the head with a dildo. Quite brutally. Finally, as they X-ray you to discover the damage done to your poor, twisted bones in the week's battles and batteries, you discover to your horror but not (at this stage) surprise that your legs are in fact made of dildos. Not for the first time this week, you consider the wisdom of having bought a house built on the grounds of an abandoned Navaho dildo factory.

Scorpio: A thoughtful time for you, Scorpio. Indeed, struck with reflection at lunch one day, you suddenly question the wisdom of consuming your sandwich. Why not trade it? You could make a profit, perhaps, or at least find some variation from the daily grind. Hell, the interaction will be fun imagine who you might chat to, what smiles you might bring to faces with your crazy scheme! And so you do - though it's a little less glamorous than in your mind and a little more socially awkward the first time, you successfully trade your sandwich with some old geezer for slightly more than it was worth in small change. Apparently the guy really liked cheese and pickle. You try again and this time take a gamble! You get a large piece of ham and a scratch card. The scratch card wins! Not big, but you're suddenly up a few hundred bucks! This is your time! You continue, trading the money for a broken down car, which you trade for working car, for a beautiful truck, for a run-down garage full of junk, which you sell! Now you have enough for a plot of land! A house! With the contacts and skills you've learned, you take a huge investment chance and end up holding a controlling share in a small electronics company worth millions! As you stroll in on the first day after the company opens its brand new offices that you traded with the previous tenant for a lousy few thousand bucks, you are crushed to death by a huge box of malfunctioning dildos.

Sagittarius: You convince everybody at work that it would be relaxing and fun to all stage a giant teddy bear's picnic at lunch time. And you're right.

Capricorn: Fairly usual sort of week for you, Capricorn. Your pelvis goes invisible because of gypsies. Yep. Your mind is stolen by international butter-thieves, to pilot their time-travelling butter-wagon which they attempt to fly into the sun while holding the French President to ransom. As you do. Your wife turns out to be an illusion caused by carefully reflected photographs of a pear. Typical. You are elected the One True King of Zimbabwe, but then subsequently deposed because of a nut allergy. As per, really. All the stars really have to give you is that you might want to look at your salt intake at some point, best check now before you get the doctor moaning, right? Toodle-pip!

Aquarius: Relax in a candle-lit bath with hints of kumquat and lavender. Let the stress of the week slowly release itself as your spirit is soothed by the sound of Enya and whale-song. Enjoy a tension-soothing massage at the hands of a skilled therapist and beautician. Start to question the qualifications of the therapist as the massage gets a little unruly. Eventually realise this is no therapist, this is Enya and she's drunk. Reel with concussion as yet again, you are beaten up by Enya, who desperately needs money for smack and doesn't care how she gets it. Ahhhh, Enya.

Pisces: It's starting to look very much like your life until this point has in fact been an 8-bit video game. To be honest, the realisation comes as something of a relief. It certainly explains quite a lot. Your girl-friend's repeated abductions, the sheer quantity of discarded gold found in practically any container. The generally aggressive demeanour and 80s hairstyles of everybody you have met lately and why you've large-ly met them on architecturally repetitive streets in downtown New York, or within the equally repeti-tively-decorated lair of Dr Kang. You don't even know who Dr Kang is, and his friends keep hitting you. You stab them until they drop a piece of cooked-chicken or sometimes an apple, both of which make you feel considerably better. Oh well, back to the grind. Dr Kang isn't going to defeat himself. Time to rescue that girlfriend. Again. At least they play chip-tune music here.

∾

Ah, you return! Obese with the sweet-meats of knowledge, I can see from your rosy demeanour that you have force-fed yourself into a veritable foie gras of futurism! Excellent, excellent, you shall be absolutely scrumptious - I mean happy! Go then, go trundle around the paddock of your days, nibbling upon the fronds of chance, grazing on contemplation, never for a moment concerning yourself with the distant shrieks coming from that old grey building, never questioning the arrival of that grubby-looking van that seems to keep arriving, adorned with the faded adverts for Professor Brains' Magical Mind Meats (they're delicious)".

Play and frolic, my tasty ones, the world is yours!

For now.

24

The week of June the 11th

WELCOME, traveller!

Ah, that you should meet me at this hour, it is most unusual, yes? Indeed. The wise women saw you not and your name is not engraved upon the sacred bark of the tree of visitation. Truly, you are most unexpected. And for this, I must beg your forgiveness as obviously, were the signs and portents less oblivious to your arrival then I most certainly would have put on some trousers.

Alas, we must make the best of what we have. You seek answers. You may find them yet. Walk forward, adventurer!

~

Aries: A chimp with a cello chews your shoes while you're choosing some choons from a shrew on a choo-choo, on shrooms. A little too many drugs for a school night, don't you think, Aries? Go and lie down in the ambient hutch and drink some water. And take that silly hat off. You're not one of the Dukes of Hazard. You're not. You're NOT. No, I know, mate, but you're not. Yes, I love you too. Yes, we're all one with nature and we're all made of stars, I know, mate, but seriously, shut up and lie down. Jesus.

Taurus: Reluctantly, you peer through the curtains after hearing what you very much suspect to have been a muffled gun shot. But who would want to kill the General on such a crowded train? He had no enemies to speak of and the poor old goon was as likely as not to shuffle off this mortal coil in the next month or two anyway. You could have stopped his heart with a starting pistol. And, indeed, you did. But they'll never suspect YOU, will they, Taurus? Oh no. How could they possibly discover the concealed starting pistol in that revealing red dress? You limp slowly to the bathroom, trying to look nonchalant and spend the next hour flushing.

Gemini: Away, Gemini, away! To Venezuala, where a new life awaits you! Don't tarry, pack a bag! You can make the last flight this evening and nobody at work will even know until tomorrow when you're away, far far away, where the stars have promised you will meet your new lover, make your fortunes, be adored by millions and live a long life filled with passion! To Venezuala, away! Awa... ah. What? Yes. Ok. The stars were looking at the map wrong. They actually meant Portsmouth. Sorry.

Cancer: Sometimes it can feel for you as though you don't really live with your feet on the ground of this planet. You watch relationships and events from afar, like a distant piece of space-flotsam, gently orbiting the Earth, observing but never quite able to reach out and touch the warm, exciting people scurrying beneath you like such tiny ants, always so very busy. Which is why you came up with the Plan. You can't touch them, oh no. Too far away. They don't want to let you into their lives, they laugh at you up there, remote, lingering in the sky. "Aloof" they call you. But you can sure as hell fire poo at them with a catapult. OH YES, YOU LITTLE SONS OF BITCH-ES. LAUGH IT UP, YOU TINY HUMAN VERMIN, IT'S ORBITAL CACA-BOMBARDMENT TIME. UN-LEASH THE BUM-DOGS OF WAR! EAT BROWN PEBBLE-DASHED JUSTICE, MOTHERFUCKERS! AIIIIIEEEE!

Leo: You sit down one day with some Sunny Delight, just sipping away at it, pint after pint. As the day passes on you feel more than alright, as you sip-sippety sip at that Sunny Delight. A man takes all your money, but you put up no fight, you just smile and relax with your Sunny Delight. The police bang quite loudly but the door is locked tight, you drink Sunny Delight through the day and the night. An old man winds you in, you're attached to a kite! You've been floating and flying with Sunny Delight, he says you gave everyone such a big fright but you giggle and drool gobs of Sunny Delight. The big doors swinging shut cut out all of the light and they will not release you nor bargain your plight. You try cutting yourself but it doesn't taste right, oh my gosh how you miss drinking Sunny Delight. Sunny Delight. Sunny Delight. SUNNY DELIGHT. Look, what we're saying here is that if you drink that much Sunny Delight, you will go fucking insane. Stop it.

Virgo: Virgo. Virgo. Virrrrrrgo. OKAY! Virgo. Really? I mean, you don't care, do you? That much? You do.

Right. OK. See, the thing is, your notes are all smudgy and the stars are pretty quiet and distant and being all alien and whatnot this evening and they're really not giving anything away, so how about you have this lollipop and we just call it quits? Yeah? No. OK. Fine. Virgoooo, Virgo. Virgo. Youuuuu... you... get... Vertigo. There you are. You got vertigo, that's what happens. Everybody born from blah blah August to, mmmm, whatever in September, you're all scared of heights. Yep. Even if you fly planes, doesn't matter. Vertigo, it is. Done. That's what you get for being dicks.

Libra: Pets are in your future. The stars are very specific about this. Very specific indeed. In this instance, cats. You will go out and acquire three cats. All the same. All tiny, mewing little kittens. You will name them all Mongo. All three of them: Mongo. If anyone asks, then you tell them the stars told you they should all be called Mongo. This will bring you great luck! Amazing luck! Incredible luck! Oh, god, the luck it will bring you! You will get gold, riches, sex with somebody you quite fancy, a modest chocolate bar advertising contract, a new car and let's call it five ounces of really tip-top skunk. But they have to be called Mongo. That's all the stars stipulate. Mongo.

Scorpio: You meet Sting in a cafe. He can't stop to talk for too long, but in the brief time you spend together, he bestows upon you the gift of a magical flute that he promises you earnestly contains awesome and terrifying powers that will only be revealed to you once you the flute acknowledges you as its true master. You thank Sting profusely, though as he departs, wonder why he smells quite so much. Some time later in the day, your mother finds you practising diligently in your room, filled with certainty that you will prove to the flute that you are its master and your true potential will be unleashed. Your mother looks at you, nods wisely and extends her hand toward you. She takes the flute and says quietly that you're not allowed to go to the cafe any more because you keep coming home with flutes from that man who looks like Sting and puts flutes up his bum.

Sagittarius: This is going to be one of those Peach days, again, you just know it. Go to work, all you've remembered to take for lunch is a peach. Sit down to work on your computer, it's turned into a peach. Complain to the IT department, nobody answers. Walk to the helpdesk and all of the staff are peaches. Toss a coin into the air and it comes down on the side marked with a peach. On the way home, you see a man wearing a peach-coloured suit, selling apples. Desperately, you enquire how much. 50p each. P each. Peach. Peach. Peeeeeeeeeeeaaaaccccchhh.

Capricorn: Your friend, a Sagittarius, is having the Peach Dream at work again. You casually lean over and Facejack them, then steal their lunch. A single, delicious peach. The rest of your day proceeds much according to plan. You swim with apes. Wrestle with dolphins. Idly consider relocating to Wolverhampton. By the time the night falls, you feel quiet and relaxed, ready for a good evening's sleep and a fresh new start in the morning. If there's a moral here, it's simply that it's good to nick fruit off of people while they're asleep.

Aquarius: This is a complex week for your heart - and anyone you're currently boinking. In short, your genitals become invisible and your nipples begin to emit a loud, siren-like noise every time you get aroused. To begin with, this is amusing but soon enough, tempers wear thin. If you're the sort to plan ahead, well, this would be a very good week indeed to stock up on skin-tone latex genital-paint and tiny, woollen nipple-silencers.

Pisces: Lady luck smiles upon all Pisceans during this time of year! Owing to the position of the stars and the strong link between Pisces and breadcrumbs, you will be immediately hailed by all who meet you as the Princess of All Biscuits. Strangers will stop you in the street to admire your wafers. Friends won't be able to resist a sneaky lick when they think you aren't watching. You are, of course, but why not let them have a bit of fun? In fact, why don't you join them? Go on, tuck in! You're delicious! Your power animal is: The Garibaldi.

~

Well, well, I see you survived the Trial of the Woods and the Testing at the Centre of the Mountain. And perhaps you came upon the lizard-guardian Grunthar while he was sleeping, yes? Indeed, you seem to have slipped by him unmolested.

That is well, young adventurer. Perhaps, then we will meet again.

Now, my scrying bowl is filled only with visions

of your hook-slinging, so I bid you a good morrow and ask that you briskly cock off.

Go on. You heard. Don't let the portcullis hit your balls on the way out.

25

The week of June the 18th

Sweet Christ, mister Stubtoe, the sound of those badgers is getting damned loud. Impudent little swines, I fear we may be forced to fetch them a swift slap on their nipples if they don't quieten down. FETCH MY BROOM.

Wait. Return the broom to its closet, good mister Stubtoe. It was not the badgers in the basement after all, but something altogether less comely.

Welcome, you lithe young crab-apple of a thing. I suspect you're here for wisdom, yes? Wisdom and a cup of delicious cider? Lurking in the shadows around my door. I'm sure you didn't think we'd see you there, slinking about with your sticky fingers.

But oh, we'll see. We'll definitely see, that's a promise.

~

Aries: While passing through your local supermarket, you are suddenly gripped by a desire to taste the

nectar of your childhood, a delicious, room-tempera-
ture glass of Lupin Squash. To your surprised delight,
you find some, hidden away behind the Vimto and
Robinson's, in a dusty old bottle. Gleefully, you take
it home and are happily gulping down your second
pint before the memory hits you like a brick in the
tits. There was never any Lupin Squash. That was the
code word you used for when the dog tried to have sex
with grandma.

Taurus: You spend a pleasant afternoon musing on
the etymology of the word 'circumference'. "Circum",
you think, idly " - from the Latin for fat-knacker", you
suppose. And "-ference", you hazard "from the Dutch,
literally meaning a Ferret named Terrence". You are a
twat, it turns out, and know nothing of words.

Gemini: If you go down to the air-strip today, you're
in for a big surprise! If you go down to the air-strip today, you'll never believe your eyes! For every General
that ever there were is naked and horny and calling
you "Sir!" - today's the day the Generals get their genitals whipped.

Cancer: Chelmsford. Half past four. Overcoat.
Marmalade. Antique Sheath. These words will have
meaning for you only moments before it is too late.
Your power animal is: Fondue.

Leo: A challenging week. You will be commissioned
by an old friend to paint them a piece in oils, depict-
ing an old purse which they claim to be dear to them.
Inevitably, it turns out to be Hitler's purse. You are
shunned roundly. Colleagues ignore you and small
children steal your lunch. Possibly the preceding

commissions, turning out (as they did) to be Hitler's moustache, spine and favourite aunt, could have tipped you off as to the nature of this latest work. Deep down, you begin to concede that you just like painting Hitler.

Virgo: A funeral is in the air. Somebody very near to you has done a powerful wrong in the eyes of a great spirit whose fury will not be slow to make itself felt. You slowly spoon pints of fresh yoghurt into the underpants and nod. Yes. That's what they'll think. It was dead Uncle Henry. Back for revenge. With the yoghurt. In the pants. He always did really like pants. That's what they'll think, all right. Pants.

Libra: Yet again, Keith Chegwin mocks you with his knowledge of astrophysics. You consider changing your car-pooling arrangements, or perhaps even requesting a change of department at work, but it's no good. Chegwin follows you, relentlessly. From job to job, town to town. Over mountain and dale. Your eyes screwed up, holding on tight to your lover, you hear her quietly mumble something about Neptune and sit bolt-upright in bed. Chegwin, again. Dressed as your wife. In the morning, he makes small-talk about comets while you try to swallow down your cornflakes. You rush to the bathroom and splash your face with cold water. When you look up, it's no surprise. You're Keith Chegwin. You always have been. You saunter off happily, mumbling something about solar winds.

Scorpio: It strikes you as increasingly possible that the owner of your company may have said something other than the words "booty call". You zip up and re-open Microsoft Excel. Shhh. Act like nothing happened.

Sagittarius: It is your second day in your new position as Prometheus of the Bees. You stole the gift of fire from the Gods and took it to bees, to illuminate their culture and works and free them from darkness. You made peace between Humanity and the fearsome Bee Nation by arranging a marriage between the human Katy Price and Thrungar, the Stinged One. Soon, you will join them in the ultimate Bee Ritual and take a Bee Wife of your own. As the bees see it, though, you set fire to some bees, stapled a large bee to a picture of a stupid human woman and then tried to make love to another really confused bee. Many of the bees seem disappointed with this entire situation, even the ones you furnished with tiny hats. They politely ask you to leave.

Capricorn: There is nothing wrong with your plans to build a Lego Volvo. Everyone likes Lego. Everyone likes Volvos. It'll be FUCKING SWEET. Anyway, fuck them. What are they going to make? A fucking Sticklebrick Renault Picasso? Oh, fucking yes.

Aquarius: Your attempts to gain larger, more environmentally-friendly eggs for Hertfordshire, by enlarging the exit from which the eggs appear is, as it turns out, misguided. It is some considerable time until people allow you to forget about what they come to refer to as the Hemel Hempstead Hen-Dremel Genocide.

Pisces: You are the queen of tiny pies. You are the queen of tiny pies. You hear them tell their tiny lies, but still they rest beneath your eyes, these miniature steak and liver sighs, the whispering pastries criticise BUT THEY CAN'T SEE YOUR BAKED SURPRISE, YOU'LL CRUSH THEM WITH YOUR SAVOURY THIGHS! HOW DARE THEY TELL THESE TINY LIES?! YOU'LL SMASH THEIR LIDS AND GOBBLE THEIR KIDS AND SLICE AND DICE THEIR PASTRY EYES! You are the queen of tiny pies. You are the queen of tiny pies. You ARE the queen of tiny pies.

~

Ho hum, tiddly-tum the wheels turn and back you come. Hurry now, my young scrumper of knowledge. Jump over the stile and run home with your arms full of truths before mister Stubtoe gets out of the gate with his hounds. They're not trained to kill, oh no! Or main, or hardly bite at all. But they are really quite lonely and it's awful dark outside.

I'd be getting home, if I were you, young 'un.

Mister Stubtoe. See them to the door.

26

The week of June the 25th

Alright, you slags.

So, you want some fucking Eldritch wisdom, do you, you fucking toilet?

Right, then. Strap this on, you pelvis. I've got your inevitable future harmonies right here, on a till-receipt marked "SOFT COUNTRYSIDE MUPPET".

~

Aries: You buy some fings off of a market. You are not a slag. Life rewards you. You shut your fucking mouth and get lost.

Taurus: You turn out to be one of them city types, flouncing about with your grey woolen coat thing, probably talking about markets, but as it turns out, you mean complex financial instruments. Which makes you a SLAG. You are roughed up good and proper by a proper fucking Cockney gent. He calls you a toilet. You are grateful. You slope home to your fucking penthouse apartment or something and reflect upon why you don't spend enough times in boxing gymns in Bethnal Green. An epiphany strikes, and you are a fucking slag for knowing what that word means. You resolve to stop wetting yourself at night, but are doomed to failure. Some kids laugh at your stupid suit. You suspect this is going to happen more in future, which represents the only thing you got right this week.

Gemini: You are a toilet. You owe me a pony and free sovs. On meeting me in the street, my usually beneficent countenance is blighted by your obvious lack of enjoyment of East Enders. I call you a slag. As testament to my ability to accurately assess humans in a cold-reading situation, you shrug a bit and say something like "I'm terribly sorry". I punch you in the mouth and we say no more about it.

Cancer: Mincing into the joint, you inadvertently spill Large Bob's pint. Fortunately, he is spectacularly high from accidentally ingesting what appears to be the only remaining wrap of decent charlie in the West End. Large Bob attempts to sell you a screen play which you foolishly criticise. The rest of the week is spend bleeding in one of them BUPA places your sort apparently can afford. You are, somewhat predictably in the "slags ward". Your cockney nurse "accidentally" writes the wrong thing on your chart, resulting in your fast-tracking to a medically-questionable bollock-ectomy.

Leo: You inexcusably fail to know either that Arsenal recently lost to the Yids and unaccountably receive a series of punches to the throat. On reflection, you realise that you are most likely either a slag or one of them foreign lot. Your apologies mean nothing to anyone and you are overcharged for some T-shirts.

Virgo: You are from the North. While potentially threatening to a proper Southerner, with your advanced knowledge of poverty and having a fight with some bricks in a ditch, your inability to navigate the London Underground leads you to be (arguably) confused with a homeless person. Proper people, who live in London and have jobs and watch the football spit on you and assume that you're Polish or from one of them countries what speak English but talk funny. Like Ireland. An old lady offers you some money to do her drive, which you inexplicably refuse. You are beaten brutally by the old dear and spend the evening constituting a drain on good, honest Southern resources, like the Acton A&E. A comprehensive diagnosis eventually reveals that you are, somewhat unsurprisingly, a slag.

Libra: You are a slag, because you stood there and watched your Virgo mate get properly slapped up like a nonce. French Tony pretends not to notice you for long enough for you to slink off and try to call the filth. At which point, the natural order of things asserts itself and a kindly young scrote on a BMX relieves you of your fucking ponce-laden Jesus Phone.

Scorpio: LEAVE IT.

Sagittarius: SLAG.

Capricorn: You are from the South. While not born within the sound of Bow Bells, your ability to identify toilets and talk about people who look funny immediately in front of them, in the incorrect assumption that everyone else on the carriage was also unable to complete a GCSE serves you well. You mistakenly believe the EDL to be a post-graduate qualification. East Enders is on and you can identify with the nuanced knife-crime sub-plot, though doing so causes you to suspect you may be some sort of toilet and/or slag. You have a nice, relaxing fight with a toilet, which you call a slag. Order is restored and you awaken covered in fox piss. You are summarily pronounced Mayor.

Aquarius: You are Turkish. You have are a prominent AI specialist with a Masters in Natural Language Generation. You work unreasonable hours cleaning office spaces for people who drive poxy little cars emblazoned with the name of the fuck-awful property-management company they managed to be born into while wistfully dreaming of a life in which less people called you a toilet. The improvised explosive device you created detonates according to your specifications, levelling the toilet block of Arsenal's home ground, leaving nothing but slag. Due to a universal connection he will never truly understand, the powerful irony causes Large Bob to shit himself quite explosively outside of Poundland. Monks in Finsbury park note this but continue to meditate.

Pisces: A complicated month asserts itself upon your life-matrix. Negative toxic feeling-orbs threaten to impinge upon your delicate mental duvet, but you are able to muster your soul-animal and chase off these weak heart-poisons. You drink a refreshing yoghurt and feel at peace. A man calls you a slag and you immediately toilet. All is well.

~

Right then. That'll be ten large, you fat bitch.

No, shut it. You still owe me a Wenceslas from the dogs last Thursday gone. Don't fuck me around, you fucking Belgian, I'll have Large Bob investigate your Enterprise level encryption strategy as soon as look at you. Once he cleans himself up a bit, obviously. Narsty.

Yeah, well, then. Next week, innit.

You bring that fucking dental floss, or I'll cut your iPhone right up the Pimlico.

Apple and bastards.

I'm off down the Grattan Winter Catalogue (1994-1995).

You know.

Grattan Catalogue (1994-1995). Pub.

Slaaaag.

27

The week of July the 2nd

Night-time falls across the forest and the animals of Dobbin Wood gather together to listen to the wise old Badger tell his tales.

Badger is very old and very wise! He knows all of the stories that have ever been told in the forest and some say that in the depths of his set, he communes with the spirits and learns stories that haven't even come to pass.

But what's this? Oh dear. It seems that wise old badger has been drinking from the puddle next to the old, discarded car battery and has gone quite, quite insane. Some of the smaller animals run away in fear, but the more tenacious few stick around to listen to Badger's stories. Or perhaps, to wait until he passes out and they can feast upon his entrails.

Hark, what stories will wise, mad Badger spit from his blood-flecked lips, tonight?

~

Aries: C'mere, you! Filthy little otters, you are! I can smell your eyes! Come here and let me rub myself against you! My belly is all itchy and covered in scabs! Come here, you blighter, I want to taste your special places! I'll only eat you up a bit! Just a tiny bit! Stop crying and come here, you horrible little otter, I hope you get tangled up in the electric fence! Yeah, that's what's coming for you! The fence and the metal taste and the bees in your heart! BEES IN YOUR HEART.

Taurus: Hur hur hur hur. I seen you, Taurus. You thought I didn't, but I stood dead still and my nose and eyes blended into the foliage and I seen you! You've been putting your nethers in Mrs Squirrel's hidey hole and I seen you! Haaa hahahahaha. An owl putting his bits in a squirrel! Funniest thing I ever saw! Now, come down here, let's talk about it. Let me sniff your gizzards a bit. Just a little bit. Hur hur hur hur hur. Right up Mrs Squirrel.

Gemini: Ah, dark things. The darkness descends, it does. There is no future for you. Not here, not now. Make your peace with the big dark weasel what lives under the bridge, for you will see him soon. Black! Black, dark, grim blacky blackness is all I see and smell. It does smell a lot, actually. Like a badger's arse if I'm not mistaken. Ah, that'll be that, then. I started inspecting my arse and forgot and left my head there for a while. That might be why it's dark. Come here, I want to chew on your brush.

Cancer: What's that? I can't hear you. Come here and talk into my mouth. Go on. I've got ears in my teeth, you know. And I spit through my elbows. Anyway, it's all going to be a series of lovely surprises for you, my little deary. Love life, prosperity, health, you name it.

The wise spirit gods of the forest are looking after you this week. Until you end up getting your nipples bitten off by a narsty great badger, that is! Come here and give us a lick, you can't hide from me forever.

Leo: I think I can see snowflakes drifting about. At this time of year! Snowflakes, who would have thought? Anyway, yes, you want the future, do you? You're going to a very interesting time down the chicken-coop, if you know what I mean. Old Farmer Stevens is getting slow, I dare say you'll get half his chickens before he can find his gun tonight. Just eat 'em though, I would. If you keep putting your doo-dar in their stumps, he's going to catch you eventually, mark my words.

Virgo: YOUR EYES SMELL OF PEANUTS. Give me some jam. Jam, jam jam jam jam jam jam. JAM.

Libra: One sunny day, probably a Tuesday (it had that sort of feel to it in the air), old Mrs Tigglewanger decided she would take her washing down to the stream to give it a scrub. "What a beautiful day", she thought to herself as she hummed and skipped her way down to the bank near to the stream. No sooner had she set up her little stool and wash-board and begun to scrub scrub scrub at Mr Tigglewanger's dirty long-johns than a giant wolf popped up out of nowhere and gobbled her face off. There's a lesson in there for you.

Scorpio: I'll do you a trade. A trade, I tells you. One story for a morsel to eat. Your friends have been a little too quick and wise for my ways and I haven't been able to nibble at any of them at all so far. If you bring me that little Aries bugger, I'll let you go and give you a story. There's a good 'un. You wouldn't leave Mr Badger to starve would you, now? Run along. Don't gobble their eyes before you bring 'em back, they're the best bits.

Sagittarius: Odd times for you, my friend. You discover that a nearby owl, WHO SHALL REMAIN NAMELESS has been popping his dirty little feathery dingle-dangle into your fine lady-squirrel's furry fuzz-hole and this makes you a very angry little squirrel indeed. Very angry. So angry that you might consid-er... vengeance? Oh yes. You could take down an owl. Just wait in the right place, outside his nest, just as dusk is falling. Then BAM! Drop from the sky and rip his beak off! Owl for supper! 'Course, there's a lot of eating on an owl, if you did, I could always help you out. Go on. Bring us a bit. Doesn't have to be a good bit, I don't care. I'm a fucking badger. I could murder a bit of anus to go with these shallots, I really could.

Capricorn: Your mate the squirrel's leaving his hol-low alone this evening. You could have all his nuts away. You could probably do your business all over his bedroom before he got back. Rest your little wea-selly balls on his acorn lamp-shade, that's right, really have a laugh with it! Hahahahaha, imagine his face, that stupid, furry little bastard. Let me lick your eye-lids. Go on.

Aquarius: I think that shiny water's starting to do for me, you know. This may be my last story, the very last one I tell. Come over and sit with me. I'll make it a good story, as it's my last. Let me whisper it to you. It all began on a silvery night, deep in the dark, dark forest. GOTCHA! YUM!

Pisces: Mmmmm, delicious. Eyes and entrails, can't beat 'em. You want a bit? Yeah, tuck in, it's lovely. I think his gizzards are over there. I wouldn't take all day about it, mind, your eyes are starting to smell quite tasty as well. I could do with a pudding.

~

Old Mr Badger got his tea-time treat in the end, it seems.

And we all got stories. Well, some of us got stories. Some of us got spattered with bloody entrails and the remains of our neighbours as old, wise, mad, terrifyingly ferocious Mr Badger ripped their tiny minds out with his claws and chomped their little bones up, laughing and swearing as he went.

He seems like he's full, now, I can just hear him sicking up what's very probably the gizzards of little Timmy Watermouse over by that dock leaf. I suspect he'll want a lie down for a while now, then most likely wake up needing another drink from the shiny water. He does love it so.

Fare ye well, dear friend, keep your pelt clean and come back again soon.

28

The week of July the 9th

Salutations, greetings, well-met and "hear me now, rude-boy".

Transmissions from the Horse Nebula have begun anew. Behold, the following data-burst, fresh futures emitted from the cold, galloping vastness beyond the spiralling arms of Gunt.

Plunge the data-barb into your throbbing time-hose. Glug deep from the truth-soup and understand.

~

Aries: Your striking resemblance to Ghandi has always been something you've just lived with. But the question remains: how come you score all the chicks?

Taurus: Ah, another fine day in which to await your inevitable stardom. You don your obnoxiously expensive headphones and set off down the street, singing loudly to yourself. You get on the bus and continue to sing. How cool you look! You can tell everyone shares this opinion. Off to Tesco and you are surrounded by future-fans. It's likely their scowls and shaking heads are due to being unable to hear your musical stylings, so you crank up the volume. A pregnant lady jumps and drops her shopping. Two small children hide behind the legs of their dad as one of them starts to cry. You pick up some Findus Crispy Pancakes and head home, melodiously. As you round the corner to your flat block, a juggernaut mounts the pavement and crushes you instantly into a fine paste. Absolutely nobody in the entire world cares.

Gemini: A brand new moustache? Daring! Two moustaches? Woah there, lady, I mean... jesus, wait a second... THREE moustaches? This is getting out of hand. Oh my god. And yet, somehow, you really manage to pull-off five moustaches. Looking good!

Cancer: You go on a day trip to Bognor Regis and inadvertently enter a time-bubble in which you are transported to the 1940s, yet somehow your mobile phone still works. You use your mobile browser to consult Wikipedia, granting you a powerful informational advantage over the people native to this time period. Within hours, you are widely considered to be a bloody nuisance.

Leo: Today is the day to recreate Angry Birds using small dogs, catapults and swimming pools. You achieve a highscore and nearly drown next-door's Shih Tzu.

Virgo: You spend much of this week contemplating the sexual awakening of an Ewok.

Libra: Bacon permeates all you see and do. Its aroma fills your nostrils, wafting from the piles of bacon you have built around your house. Soon, your meat fortress will be complete and you will stand at its parapets, bedecked in a garland of sausages, screaming your defiance to the vile nation of the Potato People. Historians record the brutal conflict that ensues as "delicious".

Scorpio: While enjoying some excellent fondue, you receive a deeply troubling telegram. It is from Hitler. He is still alive. He has developed time travel. He's also pretty furious. And you owe him a packet of Monster Munch.

Sagittarius: A canon ball drops into your garden. Shortly followed by an anvil. Several horse-shoes nearly hit you in the face and, as you bravely leave the house to investigate, a delightful reproduction Norman helmet hits you squarely in the genitals. Cupid, it seems, is abroad and has shot his arrow into the heart of the local blacksmith. He likes you real good, prepare for a brutal wooing.

Capricorn: Money will be interesting this week, in that all of yours will turn to fudge upon contact with oxygen. While it remains in your bank account, this is no problem and buying goods over the internet seems to be A-OK, but as soon as you make a withdrawal, KERPOW! Fudge. The bank claims this is a temporary glitch, but refuses to refund you.

Aquarius: You enter a revolving door at a large company at the same time as a small gentleman wearing a bowler hat. Both of you have such impeccable manners that neither of you can bring themselves to leave first and so you revolve ad infinitum, in accordance with Debrett's theory of Conservation of Angular Politeness. After two long days, the police hire a man from a marketplace to roughly barge you both out of the way while talking loudly about somebody "owing him a monkey", thus the cycle is broken.

Pisces: Burka. Phil Collins album. Ten pints of Heinz mulligatawny soup. This is going to be intense.

~

Alas, this is where the datagram ends. A pity, as our expectations were that this most-recent mind-blast might contain darker wisdom yet - a cure for all illness, a way to message the dead, or the incantation that banishes Justin Bieber.

Woe. But no woe is for evo, mofo. We cast the dice back into the eyes of the space-horse and await its filthy breath once more.

Until the clip-clopping returns, dear friends. Milli Vanilli to you all.

29

The week of July the 16th

My good man! Or perhaps woman? Whichever of either you are today (I can't exactly tell right now) it matters little, it's always a pleasure to see you! I assume you'll be wanting the usual, yes? A seat near the window, a little privacy and some of our very, very special biscuits...

Do come through, right this way.

~

Aries: She will not love you, even if you manage to insert the entire lettuce. She just wants to see how far you'll shove it up there before you realise. Pull it out before it goes in too far.

Taurus: Somebody significant will visit you this week. Their name will contain the letter "S" and they will have a face and two buttocks. You will talk to them about important subjects, and when they leave you will feel substantially more at peace with the world. Breathe in and out, slowly. Remember to laugh at the little things in life. It's good to see your dealer once in a while.

Gemini: Lemon Curd. Cheese Curd. What other things have curds? This will frustrate you enormously. Almost like that whole situation with the mongers. Why do people even make these words?

Cancer: You must learn to relax more this week. When on public transport, take a few moments to close your eyes and centre yourself. The busy world around you can easily be allowed to simply melt away, leaving you in a light, calm state of self-awareness that will last for the rest of the day. Really, you just need learn how to do this without habitually soiling yourself and you're in business.

Leo: Following a conversation with colleagues, you resolve to teach yourself JavaScript. While attempting to understand how to index into an array, 4096 small crabs make their way into your trousers. You are so distracted that you inadvertently become good at Perl.

Virgo: The itch that had been developing on your elbow turns out to be a life-size birth-mark in the shape of a penguin. Exactly as you expected.

Libra: You uncover the terrible truth that has haunted you ever since your recent house-move: everybody in your street is stealing and wearing your socks. They have some kind of vacuum pipe system and they get them while you sleep. The good news is that they don't know you're onto them. Revenge must be swift and brutal.

Scorpio: Wake up. Long for some tiramisu. Go to work. Daydream about tiramisu. Lunch-time, imagine what it would be like to consume a magnificent tiramisu all to yourself. After work, walk home, push tiredly through the front door and call to your wife. She has missed you and excitedly drags you away to your bedroom, where your love-making is passionate and intense, desperate and wanton. But still, deep down, you're really just thinking of tiramisu.

Sagittarius: After three hours hours on the phone, you eventually discover that your corporate IT department is in fact run by spiders.

Capricorn: When you were young, you fancied Daphne, but as you grew and discovered more about the world, about people and yourself, that you finally began to fancy Velma instead. Which makes it rather confusing that you now categorically fancy Daphne again. Weird.

Aquarius: Try spending a week answering all significant questions with the phrase "I do it for the punani."

Pisces: A thousand tiny whelks surround you in your house made out of tiny skulls. The sky is darkening and you suspect it's going to be because of potato peel. AGAIN. That's the least of your worries, though. In the distance, you can hear the sounds of an angry badger. Angry... and horny.

~

You've finished! So soon? Excellent, excellent.

I trust your belly is full and your spirit sated?

I'll add it all to your account. Be seeing you again soon, I trust?

Oh yes... Do mind the step as you leave, our patrons are sometimes still a little distracted by the biscuits as they begin their journey home.

30

The week of July the 23rd

ONIONS! GEEEEEET YER ONIOONS!

Alright, mate, pound of onions is it? Eh? You want what? Dark equine wisdom from beyond the Thworpian Disturbances? Oh, bloody hell, keep your voice down will you, they'll all bloody want it. Look, go round the back and have a word with our Kev, he'll sort you out. Tell him Tony sent you.

~

Aries: You spend the week worrying about work. Do they like you? Do they accept you? Do they value your contribution to the team? Have they noticed that you keep small, ceramic garden gnomes in your under-wear? Do they hear the muttering voices that seem to come out of your mouth when you're trying to be quiet in meetings? Have they, perhaps, finally, found the remains?

Taurus: This week, you will - if nothing else - achieve a new record for the number of fingers you can get into a pickle jar at the same time. Sadly, not all of them will want to come back from the jar and a skilled jar-fondler will be summoned to free you. The pickles are, however, delicious and you immediately propose to them. Life is good.

Gemini: You obtain over 48,319 Kit Kat bars and go about constructing a rudimentary barracks. Within these walls, you train hamsters that you have dressed up as soldiers in strict drills and martial exercises, until you have in your hands a powerful army of mini destroyers. With these tiny killing machines, you finally burst out of your delicious hide-away and almost immediately annex Penge. Your invasion is bloodless and the people of Penge are fond of Kit Kat, so you can expect to be their democratic ruler some time by the middle of next week. If you can get the hamsters back in their harnesses.

Cancer: Your nemesis develops a time-travel device and uses it to wage a profoundly subtle psychological war against you. Using his terrible new powers, he goes back into the past and changes the script for the TV show "Diff'rent Strokes", so that the catch-phrase of the little chap who's always standing around looking cute is suddenly now "Whutch talkin' bout, *Bernard?*". This get *really* annoying.

Leo: If you're going to spend the day wearing only your pants, you figure you might as *well* rub fresh lemon juice into your nipples. Pretty much constantly throughout the day. You feel zingy! You are eventually killed by a massive pancake which falls from the sky, screaming the word "VENGEANGE".

Virgo: When you are alone, you wish for company. When you are with company, you seek solitude. When you are busy, you look forward to rest, yet when you are idle, you crave to engage in new works. When you are poor, you dream of riches. And when you are rich, you spend it all on parsnips. You are a conundrum.

Libra: Take the day off. Buy yourself a lizard. Nurture it, sing to it, call it Susan. Take the lizard for a walk. For a run! For a FLY! Wear the lizard as a hat. Take the lizard out to dinner. Laugh and joke with the lizard. Confide in the lizard. Unburden yourself to the lizard. Return home, finally and put the lizard in its tank. A beautiful day. A beautiful friendship. A beautiful lizard... Do not, under any circumstances, have sex with the lizard.

Scorpio: Owing to a mix-up with the inter-office post system, you inadvertently send a rather angry letter which is accidentally delivered to a Bolivian drugs cartel, renowned for decapitating their rival gangs and leaving the heads outside their headquarters as a warning to their enemies. In this instance, though, they apologise profusely and immediately send you the new version of the logo you demanded. You're getting good at these stroppy letters.

Sagittarius: Is it truly the venom of the snake that bites us, which kills us? Or is it our conscience and the weight of our deeds? It's the snake. Go to the doctor before that falls off, they're not meant to be that colour.

Capricorn: While standing in the shower, you suddenly become aware that you have an unexpected third elbow.

Aquarius: It is time. Pack the suitcase. Send the email. Get in the car. Deliver the message. Perform the job. Collect the ticket. Take the plane. Disappear. They must never know that you have always secretly lived inside Terry Wogan.

Pisces: The day has been long, but now you can relax. Tiny puppies kiss and tickle you. Fish swim lovingly around your knees. The post-man brings you some Ovaltine, then drifts away languidly into the sky, whistling "Just a Spoon Full of Sugar". It's possible, you think, that you might have gone insane, but if you have, you are reconciled to simply enjoying it. Justin Bieber hums lullabies while you get comfy. You playfully shoot him in the mind with a semi-automatic rifle and all is peace and tranquility. Perhaps next week will be better. It's been months since you had the Hammers Dream.

~

All sorted, are ya? Good lad. Now do us a favour and take some of these onions off my hands for me will you? They bloody stink. Of onions, obviously, but still.

ONIONNNNNNSssah!

31

The week of July the 30th

Dearly beloved. We are gathered here today to receive divine wisdom and guidance from our majestic Lord, the giant space horse in the sky, that answers only to the name THWAMSHED BALTHOG N'WOP 7.

Let us bow our heads in confusion and await his terrible breath upon the backs of our necks. Amen.

~

Aries: You are asked to cease attending your local church after a particularly enthusiastic fund-raiser party. It seems the rest of the flock were not wholly behind such ideas as "dirty communion", "competition bible-fucking" or "pin the merkin on the virgin". Off the record, the vicar reveals this was the best Sunday afternoon he's ever had, but you suspect he might still be high from what you put in the wafers.

Taurus: The Lord visits you in a dream. It is a sexy dream. You spend the entire night dreaming about being viciously, arse-rendingly power-banged by Jesus and a few angels with strap-ons. When you awaken, the pages of your bible are stuck together.

Gemini: Your neighbourhood becomes a dangerous place to walk at night. The stars recommend staying to well-lit streets and avoiding travelling alone. No longer welcome in their place of office, anarchic bands of priests have been discovered wandering the highstreets and alley-ways of most cities. Some attempt to sell their bodies to swell their own parish coffers, while others talk with their fists, either assailing those who walk off the beaten path, or in unregulated underground boxing matches. Do not approach these individuals. The will do more than beat the evil out of you.

Cancer: A scruffy but enthusiastic gentleman with a ghetto blaster approaches you in the street and causes you to seriously doubt the existence of Neil Diamond. He claims to bring the word of Dubstep to all who will hear it and encourages you to wub thy brother, as one wubs oneself. Unlike Christ, he suggests following the path of Skrillex (whose speakers died for our sins) and who, rather than curing the lame strongly encourages sickness in all forms. Skrillxians are also known to hold the Sabbath holy, and, in His name, to keep it Large.

Leo: You would do well to spend this week contemplating the Holy Trinity: drinking beer, smirking tabs (liek) and of course a nice curry, the nah.

Virgo: Throughout the week, events arise such that you are strongly minded of the parable of the good Samaritan. Primarily, you are strongly ignoring it as you kick those who are down, take from the pockets of the poor and unselfconsciously shit on the graves of the innocent. A week before pay-day, all bets are off. If they wanted to keep their watches, they shouldn't have shook your hand.

Libra: Being endowed as you are, it is perhaps little surprise to you that Jesus chooses to return not as a man or a woman per se, but instead manifests Himself in your undercrackers. Similarly, you remain unphased by the fact that He begins to speak from down there. Your sexuality and faith are both sufficiently robust: if this is His will, let it be done. It does seem a smidge uncouth, however, when on the weekend, you're overheard telling somebody at the bar to "Gowan and give us a lick down there, I've got the Son of God in me pants".

Scorpio: Recently, you've been feeling as though your life is going to hell, but now it categorically, truly is. Good news! (Depending on your faith) - Satan himself has apparently stumbled on your profile on LinkedIn and likes what he sees! You've been summoned to the office of the Big Red Dude downstairs, where he hopes to make you an offer you won't refuse. Fully heated, all the best music and the view is a scream. The only thing you find hard to swallow (ugh)... they all use Macs.

Sagittarius: You find yourself temporarily in Wales, where you are arrested for claiming David Bowie to be the Lord. Of course, Bowie then arrives and demonstrates that he is, so it all turns out okay. For bonus points, he's wearing those tights off of Labyrinth, leaving few in any doubt.

Capricorn: The stars are not clear exactly what happens to you during this week, particularly not what it is you do that causes your expiration. We're jolly sorry about that, truly we are, we'd love to help you dodge the bullet so to speak (we're not saying it's a bullet, that's metaphor). They are, however, adamant that when you croak (and you will) you are almost immediately reincarnated as an otter.

Aquarius: Friends summarily declare you to be the Vegan Anti-Christ and you embark upon a reign of terror around South London. Some days later, you wake up in the middle of a traffic island near Pimlico, being poked by a traffic warden. You are surrounded by hundreds of apparently crucified parsnips. You regret nothing.

Pisces: It's Sunday afternoon and yet again, rather than attending church, you're watching brutal, uncompromising pornography. Part way into the fifth or sixth abuse of the day, it occurs to you that if only the grot you watch were themed around genuine biblical messages and performed by clergy, instead of feeling guilt and sexual horror, you could simultaneously pleasure yourself and please the Lord. Onlookers report the "genuinely crestfallen" look on your face as you are marched from the synagogue and hurriedly driven home by red-faced family members.

~

Our father, who art a massive space-horse, THWAMSHED BALTHOG N'WOP 7 be thy name. Thy kingdom come, Thy will be done, in Wood Green as it be in heaven.

We hope your prayers have been, at least in some way, addressed.

Please remember that our heavenly donation plate accepts VISA, Paypal and Bitcoin.

32

The week of August the 6th

Good afternoon, come in, sit down. Now, what exactly is it that you've been having a trouble with? My dear aunt Jemima, yes, I see now. That's practically about to fall off.

NURSE! Bring me 50cc of Eldritch Wisdom. And a bucket. You? You'd best drop your trousers and cough, this will only hurt a little bit...

~

Aries: You seem to be running a fever. The warmth from your soul is channelling directly up through your spleen, giving rise to some quite undesirable contusions and maladies. Try to reduce your temperature by putting a wet flannel on your sunny disposition. Turn off that smile and knee the world in the plums. If you have a puppy, give it the boot. If you don't have a puppy, find one and shave it. Take some money from the next beggar you see. Deliberately start slipping small items belonging to other people into your pockets and sauntering away with an evil laugh. Excellent, you'll do well. Give me back my pen.

Taurus: Latin music appears to bring you out in the

strangest of allergies. Your body twists and shimmies in time to the beat while your nipples obey a rhythm described only by the very devil himself. Your diagnosis: You have succumbed to the Lambada (the Forbidden Dance). As usual, the solution to this problem is two-fold. A pint of ice-tea (drink quickly, then use the ice on the nipples) and an hour a day of the Wu-Tang Clan. Come back next week.

Gemini: Interesting. This is what, now? Your *third* penis in as many days, all sprouting directly from your face? Well, indeed, it does seem as though the stars have blessed you with a special gift indeed. You are Simon Cowell. There is no cure. Please take this electric drill. Orally.

Cancer: Cancer. Cancer. Cancer. Try as much as I like, your diagnosis escapes me. It's almost on the tip of my tongue, but I cannot bring it to my mind. Cancer... What could be wrong with you? With your undercarriage all... yes, and your face and throat pretty much oozing the... indeed, and your lungs obviously filled with a sort of. Mmhmm. What am I to do with you? WAIT! THAT'S IT! It was staring me in the face all along! You're French. NEXT.

Leo: I can certainly see how this last week or so has been confusing for you. Your hair feeling a bit coarse and straw-like? Yes. Cooler, more difficult to keep warm recently, particularly in the rain? Quite. And you feel a little shorter and closer to the ground than you're accustomed to? Exactly so. And last, but not least, you feel very much as if a small family from Essex is living inside you for the duration of the Easter school holidays? I have it. Nothing could be clearer.

You are in fact a small holiday cottage in Purfleet. It is, I'm afraid, congenital. Try to look after your thatch.

Virgo: You have obviously not gone dancing naked in the rain enough recently. Go on, put Blue Perl on the old iPod, find some way to wear the iPod naked and get out there. You're only getting older, this isn't going to get any easier. Just for ten minutes, it can be at night if you like. Get it out of your system, let somebody post a blurry picture of you flopping about on the high street on Twitter with your tackle out, you'll feel right as... well, rain.

Libra: If my nose doesn't deceive me, you've been watching rather too much Jeremy Clarkson recently. Give me your elbow, let me have a sniff. Yes, I thought so. Leather pads. Really, at your age. If you take my advice, you'll drive an electric car twice a week for the next six months and start listening to Radio 4 before the perm and the self-righteousness really set in. Snap out of it!

Scorpio: Nothing wrong with you, nothing at all! If anything, you look quite healthy. Except that left eye, that does look a little bit odd. Let me just take a quick peek in there with my tools - don't blink, or the eye might come off. Aha. Just as I suspected. You are infected with ghosts. Yes, quite a common disease these days, though most people have the good sense to avoid having sex with Sigourney Weaver at the top of a skyscraper, or at least hose themselves down with a proton pack afterwards. Just pop one of these in your mouth and don't think of anything that could destroy the city. What is it? Oh, it's a marshmallow.

Sagittarius: There's good news and bad news. Good news: You're pregnant! Bad news: It's mostly owls.

Capricorn: Now, I've examined your urine sample and I'm slightly concerned about your diet recently. I want you to be honest and open about this, because I'm only asking for your own benefit and I really have seen it all before, but in your urine sample, I did find really large amounts of... I mean it was almost entirely composed... of urine. Have you been mostly just consuming urine? Because that's all I could find. Stop drinking urine. Ahhh. Urine.

Aquarius: Bit of a problem here. I've been on the phone to your work place and also talked to your family a little and it seems to come down to this: over the last month or so, maybe the last few years but really coming to a head this week, you've really not for even a couple of seconds successfully shut the actual fuck up, have you? It's almost like a valve went and you've just not been able to get that bit on the front of your face (in medical terms, the 'yap') to stop flapping. It's fine, it's not fatal and your family are certainly all behind you, but you are going to have to take one of these, immediately. It's a cork. Come back tomorrow, I'll put on some ear protectors, take out the cork for a few minutes while we spoon in some yoghurt or something to keep you well-nourished, then we'll pop that sucker right back in. For the conceivable future. It's for the best.

Pisces: Your skin is strangely off-colour and cool to my fingers. Your flesh yields to my firm, probing touch. Your blood seems to have taken on the viscosity of syrup, it is fragrant, delicious to me! OH VENGE-

FUL ANCIENTS - I THOUGHT I MIGHT ESCAPE, BUT COULD I FINALLY HAVE SUCCUMBED? AM I NOW ONE OF THE DARK ONES? THE NIGHTLINGS THAT LIVE ONLY FOR TERROR AND TO CONSUME VIRTUE AND LEAVE THE INNOCENT SUFFERING?! AM I... A... A VAMPIRE?! Or, no: you are in fact a delicious, ripe peach. And I am, of course, your doctor. NEXT!

~

Yes, I think that's just about got it. Though I'm going to need to bill you for a new machine after all that struggling. Anyway, we got there in the end. I'll have this thing sent off to the lab, see what they make of it. Or maybe just the incinerator, some things are best left unexamined.

I hope you feel suitably enlightened... physically, spiritually and (I dare say) financially. Don't try to answer, it'll take a while for the anaesthetic to wear off and we wouldn't want your drool all over the tiles, now.

Let the nurse know I need to see you next week. Just... waggle your eyebrows a bit, she'll get the idea. Ciao!

33

The week of August the 13th

Yet again we point our satellites into the stars, sweeping their distant depths for signal. Keenly homing in on the wisdom among the noise.

Once located, we pipe those radioactive mind-beams straight into your head using a thing we call "words" projected directly onto what you humans likely refer to as a "page".

Hold onto your trousers, my little pamplemousse, shit's about to get elliptical.

~

Aries: After spending three days locked in a cupboard, in fear of the giant hovering brain with the sharp teeth and drills, you decide that it may be time to cut down on the recreational substance abuse. The rest of the week is spent gently sucking at a rice-cake while watching children's television. Unfortunately, owing the to nature of modern children's TV, this turns out to be even more terrifying. By the end of the week, you return to the drugs and a series of hallucinations you can (at least) identify with.

Taurus: You dream of navigating a long hotel corridor in which each of the doors slams forcefully shut before you can get close. Tantalising glimpses of the contents of the rooms make you quicken your pace - it almost seems as though behind each door is another world, another future that could be yours if only you could slip across the threshold before the door is forever shut, but you can never run fast enough to make this come true. Recently, the sense of frustration has been so overwhelming that you have awoken in tears of anguish, moaning "WHY? WHY??". According to the stars, this means you are constipated. Eat more fruit.

Gemini: Work has not been going so well lately and you're developing some resentment. As a petty but spiritually-rewarding attempt to stick it to the man (as it were), you have taken up stealing office supplies. Indeed, your skill is strong in this pursuit and you are soon leaving the office each day, festooned with cables, corporate-branded USB sticks and special paper for a printer you don't possess. After some months, work security track down the missing kit to your house, but by this time, you have enough of the company's assets to stage a hostile takeover. You successfully designate your bedroom as "head office" and fire all who oppose you. Sweet.

Cancer: The stars really don't like repeating themselves, but: Never (EVER) make love to your headmaster. Again.

Leo: This plan you've been working on... creating the life-size statue of Terry Wogan entirely out of that wax you get on some kinds of small cheeses. Is it going well? The stars just wonder if you might want to, you know, just take a quick look at your priorities. You're good? It's fine? Oh, okay. Fine, then. I mean, yeah. Carry on. It's looking... really... yeah.

Virgo: After your performance last week, the stars have lost all confidence in you recently, chum. You need to up your game. You killed three clowns last week. THREE. I want you to think about that. Three. It's NOT ENOUGH.

Libra: You have always been one for deep thought and this week find yourself lost among some of the most striking questions of the human condition. Thought experiments and philosophical gymnastics lead you to ask: Are you now a man dreaming he's a butterfly? Or a butterfly dreaming it's a man? Or a man dreaming he's a butterfly dreaming he's a vole, dreaming it's a paperclip, dreaming it's the Pope, dreaming he's inside Justin Bieber? You get one of those spinning tops like they use on Inception, but when you spin it, it just turns into some eels.

Scorpio: Dogs, snakes, dogs, snakes, dogs, snakes. Pretty much the same thing, right? There ain't no way that lady can sue you for giving her a box of adorable little snake-puppies. She should learn to be more specific. Stupid blind old lady.

Sagittarius: For this week only, the stars want you to try something new. Try wearing two pears of underwear each day. That's right, one pair over the other. Whenever somebody gives you stress, the stars want you to look at them and think "Hah. You don't realise that I'm wearing two pairs of knickers, motherfucker." Though it's important to not actually say this out loud. Next week, try for three.

Capricorn: Relaxation is key to you in the forthcoming days. When you feel yourself becoming agitated or losing your sense of self, try slowly, deliberately punching the face of Justin Bieber until it becomes a sort of lightish red, with bleeding somewhere between 'steadily' and 'profusely'. If the anxiety doesn't abate, you may need to extend the punching downwards, down, down, all the way down until you're really just whomping away at his smooth, hairless balls. Keep that rhythm going for a good hour or so, if you start to tire, mix it up a little and maybe start forcing bricks up his puckered, over-privileged little back passage. Any bricks will do, but we recommend house bricks, they've really got a good heft to them. Just bend that little feller over and start loading him up. That's right. Use hammers if you need to. You should find the tension really just melts away after two or three bricks and a good, solid weekend of punching. You deserve it!

Aquarius: Your rap career really begins to blossom this week, Aquarius. Notably, your latest joint is picked up by 50 Cent's G-Unit label and receives considerable respect on the West coast. This amply increases the number of bitches looking to get down with the ol' A-Q, which is a relief given last week's disappointingly poor showing on the bitch front. Ho's are also very much on the rise in the next 2-3 days, though you are likely to smack some of them down in a disrespect-related incident by the middle of next week. Remember to be true to your shareholders and, above all things, to keep it O. G.

Pisces: Plums sing to you. An angel writes you a post-card. Six mung beans perform a stunning rock-concert for you on your window sill (and bring their own laser show!) The silence tastes like a rich mug of hot chocolate. A fluffy jumper embraces you with the charm and panache of an old lover. It is just possible that after much experimentation, you have found the absolutely perfect amount of acid to drop just before midnight on a Sunday evening with work to go to in the morning. This is going to be beautiful.

~

Transmission transmitted, my favourite hairy receiver.

I hope your mind feels soft and pampered, like a bunch of intelligent fingers that just got their nails done. Drunk with information. The way that fingers get, you know, drunk.

I'll call you a mind-taxi. Let's talk about this to-morrow, when the taste of the signal dies down.

Be residual, my friend.

34

The week of August the 20th

The planets align, the stars turn Welsh, Bob Carolgees ascends powerfully in the east. In the distance, a lemon weeps proudly, atop its leather throne.

This can mean only one thing that we have the ability to understand. It is, inexplicably, time for your Horrorscopes.

~

Aries: Due to unidentified structural issues (and/or ghosts), your house falls down. Fortunately, you are able to use all of the "bags for life" that you have obtained over the years and, using only your powerful mandibles, weave them into a rudimentary castle. You look down upon your neighbours from the parapets and clack happily as they scurry about in your shadow.

Taurus: You are surprised to discover an unexpected love of geometry. By which we mean you get caught in the supplies cupboard, making love to a polygon.

Gemini: Communications can be a bit of a problem

for you, especially at this time of year. It's always worth going the extra mile to see things through if you can. This week, it turns out that what you thought people meant by "a pint of milk" was actually what most people call "a 1989 Volvo Estate". In light of this new information, you now find breakfast hugely more convenient.

Cancer: Your experiments yield unexpected results when you discover that goths actually have considerably more receptors in their eyes than normal humans and what we perceive to be simply black is in fact a veritable profusion of almost three sorts of brown.

Leo: Relax, let yourself off the hook. Despite how you probably feel right now (and how you've been feeling for a long time, if we're honest, right?) - you're not alone. Pretty much everyone goes through a phase of being sexually aroused by Inspector Poirot.

Virgo: Open the curtains, look out into the world, allow it to blow your mind. Happiness is a 400ft tall chocolate Dalek called Percy. Don't question it. Tuck in.

Libra: If today gets on top of you, close your eyes, breathe deeply and become one with the knowledge that among the infinite parallel universes through which we all move, there is one which contains a mirror-image version of you with a really awesome moustache, firing a gun at some plums.

Scorpio: You are starting to deeply regret decisions made earlier in life. Somehow, this has led to your becoming convinced that if you eat enough beef, you will develop the ability to travel back in time. When you succeed, your first message to your younger self reads simply "less beef".

Sagittarius: There are only two rules you must hold to your heart in order to prosper this week: Money will never make you happy. Custard always will.

Capricorn: Though you seek to reconcile with your past, old troubles still linger. You are particularly haunted by the unshakable suspicion that Father Christmas secretly harboured extremely racist views toward the Chinese.

Aquarius: If you have never tried making love to the music of Jean Michelle Jarre, this is the week to give it a whirl. You will find it profoundly uplifting! Try Equinoxe! That said, try not to get your nipples stuck in the laser-harp.

Pisces: The stars see great evil before you, Pisces! Evil! EVIL! You must... oh, no, predictive text, sorry. The stars see a great anvil before you. Seriously, it's fucking amazing. Bring your hammers.

~

Madness melts away and only some biscuits remain.

Take them and depart, human child. We will speak again, soon. Rich tea, seeing as you're asking.

35

The week of August the 27th

Sing HO! And FOL DE ROL, as the mystical chants of the horse people echo through the skies. Grasp hard upon the cucumber of knowledge and prepare yourself...

~

Aries: This is the week your super-powers finally mature. Your secret power? The terrifying ability to control lint.

Taurus: You will be torn by conflicting motivations this week. On one hand, a dear family member will need your assistance and reach out to you for charity in their time of need. You are uniquely positioned to empathise with their situation and connect to them on an emotional level. On the other hand, though, there is the prospect of eating some delicious ham. You choose the ham.

Gemini: The death of a family pet will leave you contemplative and thoughtful, perhaps a little pensive for the future. When it comes down to it, was it ever really a good idea to buy nanna that racing-wasp? You remember her gleefully taking it out on walks before the accident, but now it seems contentious. Only lizards from now on, nanna. Lizards and the ape.

Cancer: Love is in the air this week. You find yourself hopelessly distracted by the attentions of a quirky young lady you see on the way to work each morning. Her cheeks, her eyes, her greenish skin, the way she appears to have the horns of a ram. The lobster she holds, like a machine gun, beneath her pale arms while tadpoles slowly orbit her face. Perhaps you should think about making some time to meet women who don't work in Hoxton. Maybe look at some porn?

Leo: As most of your family are wizards, this week will of course be a time for meeting and socialising with distant relatives at the yearly Grand Wizard's Ball. There will (inevitably) be some duelling and it's likely that several of you may die or become toads, but in the mean time, relax, let your hair down and catch up on the gossip. This year, rather than causing your enemies to explode in a shower of entrails, perhaps you might consider transmogrifying them into mice and keeping them in a tiny golden cage for ever more. Much more civilised!

Virgo: Work has been leaving you tired-out, it's as though there just isn't enough time in the day. Perhaps you should consider a holiday? More to the point, perhaps you should consider not going to Cheam all the time. It can't have escaped your notice that one of the reasons you are always rushing and late for work is that you constantly accidentally travel to Cheam, which is not where you work. Then, on the way home, the same thing: "One first class ticket to Cheam, please", and it's another two hours wasted. Stop it. Stop going to Cheam. No more Cheam. Cheam.

Libra: Are you interested in politics? This week might prove to be extremely interesting for you! If not, then perhaps you're into sport? No? Then I bet you're into books, right? Exactly! So, you're a fashion person! Suffice to say: that thing you enjoy, there will be at least some of it happening this week. Probably. Or not. Look, it's hard to tell sometimes. Just drink gin until this makes sense. That's what the stars are doing.

Scorpio: If you are thinking about going on a date this week, the stars say you should be prepared to hold back your initial judgements until you've really given them a chance to shine. Sure, so she demands you go to a Portuguese restaurant and loudly discusses her love of anal sex for the full two hours. Then there's the Niqab, you weren't expecting that, particularly from the atheist dating site. OK. Lastly, of course, there's the leopard. Nobody could have expected that, fair enough, but you seem to be getting on great. Remember that she's likely to be suffering from nerves, too - the pressure of a date can often magnify the quirks and foibles that in time, you may come to love. As a quick heads-up, though, the stars think you should know that she likes the leopard to watch while she's giving you the anal sex.

Sagittarius: Sometimes it feels like you're driving your car the wrong way down a one-way street, seeing dustbins bounce off the bonnet (maybe the occasional dog) and watching the horrified faces of friends and family gesticulating wildly to stop the car, please, for the love of God, just stop the car.

Capricorn: Earlier this week, you had a tense time, didn't you, Capricorn? That's right. While bending down to tie your shoelace, you accidentally witnessed the brutal execution of a drug dealer by a naked man wearing a Father Christmas hat. You thought you got away without him seeing, but then your work colleagues started disappearing and now you're the only one left, locked in the shed, waiting for the final moments. Uh oh, what was that sound? Look up, Capricorn. That's the last pair of balls you'll ever see.

Aquarius: THE NECROMANCER COMES! THE DARK ONE! SHE WHO ROAMS THE EARTH WEARING THE SKINS OF THE SLAIN! FLEE, CHOSEN ONE! FLEE BEFORE ALL IS LOST! YOU MUST TAKE THE FORGOTTEN PATHS INTO THE SECRET PLACES, NOW, BEFORE IT IS ALL UNDONE! TAKE THE GOLDEN WEASEL AND FLY!

Pisces: Your headaches of the last few days should be fading now, so take the time to rest your weary body and mind. Make yourself a nice warm bath. Try some delicate lemon tea. Sell everything you have and use the money to buy soufflé. Knit yourself a bear costume - don't forget to leave holes for the nipples! A tasty plate full of fried butterflies will give you the boost you need to fend off the psychic attacks to come, but don't worry about them now. Feet up, costume on, fill 'er up!

The knowledge is imparted, the singing may now cease. Additionally, you may release the cucumber... and leave!

36

The week of September the 3rd

You are tuned in to H.O.R.S.E. 103.5 FM! All space-horse, ALL THE TIME!

~

Aries: Today is just going to be one of those days where you say "Fuck it", buy all the ice-cream you can lay your hands on, put it all in your pants and saunter down the street yelling "LICK ME, YOU SWINES, I AM DELICIOUS". Don't fight it.

Taurus: You invent a technological equivalent of mp3s for smell. Much of North America is subsequently gassed by Justin Bieber's first attempted release using this medium. The world's remaining nations are not sure whether to jail you or make you king, but they do explicitly ban Lemmy from recording his planned album.

Gemini: Nourishment is important this week. To get the right balance of vitamins and nutrients, it's essential that you get your 5 portions of fruit, vegetables and midget-porn.

Cancer: "Tomorrow, tomorrow, I'll love you tomorrow!" - ah, the lyrics of Annie. If anything, you have to admit that if you'd thought about it, you were sort of warned that it would be foolish to engage the entire cast of the long-running West End theatre production of Annie in prostitution. And paying them up front? Rookie move.

Leo: For a number of days, now, you've been feeling like you've lost something. Something which you can't quite identify, but feels its absence teasing at your mind. Was it your keys? No, you have them. Did you leave your card in that cash machine? No, it's in your wallet. Maybe it was your ring, do you have your wedding ring? Yes, of course, it's where it always is, next to the hummus. Then what could it possibly be? Relax, take a deep, healing breath. It was this plum.

Virgo: Sometimes you wistfully think back on the time you both spent together in that log cabin. The quietness. The still air in the forest, broken only by the occasional rustle of twigs as a bird lands or flies away. The sound of the sea. So far from all other human existence for miles around, except for each other's company. You reflect on this delicate moment of shared solitude and think: "That was when I wanted to throttle you the most".

Libra: You're not 100% certain, but if you have to sum up how this week has gone so far, you're pretty sure you'd use the words "like being fingered by a wookie in a cagoule".

Scorpio: The people you admire in your life have all had one thing in common. Great artists, mathematicians, entrepreneurs and visionaries - all of whom have acted as inspiration and guidance to you, showing the path that you must ultimately follow. It seems obvious to you now, as you reach the destination you've long travelled toward. The one shared characteristic of all of these luminaries is, it seems, that unlike you, not one of them tried to make their living selling sculptures made from their own warm shite.

Sagittarius: This is just going to be one of those weeks when you are unfairly arrested for fisting Jedward. The law is an unlubricated ass.

Capricorn: No matter where you go this week, you must be prepared for battle. To the bathroom? Take your katana! To a meeting? Take your katana! To the grocery store? Katana? To the Katana repair-man? KATANA! Once you have mastered this important life-skill, you will find true inner-peace and shall make the journey toward contentment. THEN HIT THE CONTENTMENT WITH YOUR KATANA! KA-TANA!

Aquarius: Unavoidably, it seems that you have somehow managed to sprain your mind. Still, this is what you get for dancing with the pineapple people and playing their purple pipes. Allow the madness to seep gently into the Collector's Edition Umbongo Lunchbox of your soul. There is no need to resist, Skeletor will nibble on your dangly bits either way. Feel your thoughts slowly become pendulous, like a moist Tarantino. Slide contentedly into the infinity weasel, it is finally time to do the silent boogie. Shh-hhhh.

Pisces: Now is the time, this is the hour. Let your

career in underwater yodelling TAKE FLIGHT!

~

This week's show is sponsored by RADIO CHOW™! The ONLY chow absolutely guaranteed to make your mind go "BELGIUM!"

37

The week of September the 10th

Strange oscillations bend and warp the air around you as the magnificent space lasers of the HORSE CREATURES FROM BEYOND THRUNTAR 5 hurtle through the atmosphere and light up your mind like some kind of weird, bioluminescent MIND BULB!

The allotted time is upon us: you are their target, prepare to receive your HORRORSCOPES!

~

Aries: This is going to be a week full of highs and lows regarding your love life. Stock up on lubricant and practice touching your toes. Be wary of Spaniards with rubber gloves.

Taurus: It seems strange to think that it's been one whole year since you gave birth to a lobster, but now you can't imagine life without him. Perhaps today would be a nice day to take him out for a walk... or strap on his battle-armour and go to LOBSTER FIGHT CLUB!

Gemini: It doesn't matter which path you take, this

week, it seems as though all roads lead to Wolverhampton. That's sort of the exact opposite of what you'd want, really. Still, did you know Goldie came from Wolverhampton? Yep. And his real name is Clifford. I know! Doesn't really help, does it? The stars recommend drinking some lager and having a cry round the back of a bus shelter.

Cancer: This week, your technical skills are put to great use as you invent a new power-tool / short-range projectile weapon known only as the "Drillzooka". You don a cape and take to the streets as vigilante super-hero "The Drillzooka Kid". Within hours, you have successfully slain a rogue badger, a Volvo you suspected to be 'deeply evil' and four cartons of Umbongo. Your reign of justice is finally brought to an end when you are cornered by your nemesis, Doctor Rotter, a ten-foot tall otter, made entirely out of haunted Rawl plugs.

Leo: Your sweet tooth leads you astray this week as you pass a promotional statue of a leopard made from confectionary find yourself completely unable to avoid lapping at its liquorice balls. Delicious.

Virgo: Finally, things are starting to go your way. Your health is picking up, you feel popular and appreciated. Best of all, you finally get a letter back from the council stating that they are, at last, prepared to concede it was due to their own administrative error that you have spent the last three years classified as an "illegal Welsh immigrant".

Libra: You receive a birthday card. It's for your dog. It's not your dog's birthday. You're starting to become extremely suspicious of that card shop in town and its efforts to survive the recession. The following day, your cat returns home, wearing a medal. This, at least, can be explained by her work as a sniper in the territorial army.

Scorpio: This week, mischievous Irish folk-harridan Enya comes round where you work and starts telling everybody you've been sleeping with the photocopier. Next, she visits your parents and uses Karate on your dad. Finally, she spends an entire day following your every move in a brown Austin Allegro. The only saving grace is that at no point during this period does she actually sing. Fucking Enya! Jesus.

Sagittarius: You are forced to accept that ring-binders can't talk and don't have eyes, so the remaining possibility is that you've been drinking gin at work, again. Solution? Gin.

Capricorn: Some chaps do a poo in your handbag. You give chase and eventually confront them in an alleyway, where you strike them repeatedly about the head with the first thing that comes to hand. Oh. If you are male or simply do not own a handbag, then this week, you and a couple of friends have a little fun, when you opportunistically do a poo in somebody's handbag.

Aquarius: You are feeling particularly bulbous recently. It's possible you may have to consider taking up a sport to keep yourself in shape. Well, to keep yourself in a shape that avoids accurate description by the word 'bulbous', anyway. On the up side, your beard is really coming along.

Pisces: A fairly typical week for you, Pisces. Things begin reasonably enough, you endure a tiring week at work then head out on Friday evening to blow off some steam. When you come to, you're kneeling on a stool, covered in yellow feathers, having your nipples repeatedly flicked by Gok Wan, who you seem to be feeding Prawn Cocktail flavoured crisps. He seems pretty relaxed about the whole thing, so you finish the bag and say no more about it.

∼

The illumination passes, your spotlight dims. Slowly, the alien beams from the PLANET OF THE MIND-HORSES recedes and move on to select another subject.

Allow yourself time for this intense wisdom to sink in. Slow your thoughts and keep your brain moist as it continues to expand.

Farewell for now, until our next encounter.

38

The week of September the 17th

Succumb to the infectious groove of the hooves, dear punter. We are your Prediction Jockeys, mashing up de troot and it's time to get down with your Horrorscopes. Come follow me now, homeboy.

~

Aries: Some days, you feel as though striving for a successful life is like dangling a magnet on a string into a bucket full of hand-grenades to rescue your car keys. You know... like feeding crocodiles with your willy out... Making love to Borris Johnson? ... Look, what the stars are saying is that you're a gloomy bastard and frankly, you're getting them down. Your power animal is: Robert Smith.

Taurus: Consider spending the day barefoot. This way, you can really experience what it feels like to be universally considered a tool.

Gemini: You are about to have the most MIND-SHATTERINGLY amazing sex IN THE ENTIRE UNIVERSE. The stars don't want to spoil the surprise too much, but they do think you should start preparing for this once-in-a-lifetime event *NOW*. Start doing your stretches. Take the phone off the hook. Book yourself a recovery weekend with your preferred private medical service. Stock up on extra-slippy anaesthetising professional-grade lube and buy the largest Toblerone you can find. Those last two might have let the cat out of the bag a bit, sorry.

Cancer: It's weird, but after having both of your arms accidentally amputated and replaced with angry lizards, despite the bitter malpractice case you brought against the doctor, you're starting to really enjoy the company of the lizards. They're angry, but boy, can they cook!

Leo: This Friday, beware of Cockneys bearing gifts. No, not gifts. The other thing. SHOOTERS!

Virgo: Lately you've been sleeping poorly and it all comes down to comfort. The right mattress is crucial to a good night's sleep - getting the right support - not too firm, not too soft - really makes all the difference. Selecting one can be really hard, and let's face it, nobody likes doing hard things. But pretty much everyone likes GIN! Drink some gin while imagining a nice mattress. Phone a bed shop and really shout at them. Imagine they're to blame for you running out of gin! When they hang up, that's a cracking time for some more gin. And if you still can't doze off, hey! Drink some more gin! And some more. Go on, last bit. There we go. Now just have a nice little snooze where you are, that bed's awfully far away and it looks like it's having a nice dance with its friends. Ignore the smell of wee, everything is fine. Mmmmmm. Gin.

Libra: Finances seem to be slipping out of control this week. Don't worry, though - you can get yourself back on terra firma thanks to your latest discovery! Using your formidable research skills and impeccable logic, you are able to discover that TRAMPS' INNARDS ARE MADE OF SOLID GOLD! It's true! All the time they spend lazing around, asking for money and they've got GOLDEN SPLEENS! Get your can-opener and a bucket for the gold. It's time to go to the bank.

Scorpio: You have fond memories of your art teacher from school. They were kind and listened to your opinions, when many of the other teachers were caught up with an endless cycle of filling your head with rubbish, then testing you to see if it had fallen out. Which is why you end up feeling quite strongly ambivalent when you discover them starring in porn.

Sagittarius: At work, you discover that your line manager has left at extremely short notice and, owing to administrative complexities beyond your ken, you now report directly to a rather large goose. The goose wears a bow-tie. You call him "Mister Goose". Efficiency soars.

Capricorn: Veeeeeery little to report this week, Capricorn. If you can avoid smearing Marmite over yourself and running about the office inviting everybody to nibble at you, screaming "TONGUE MY SALTY CLEFT", it'll all work out largely fine. If you can't, you can't. Don't beat yourself up.

Aquarius: This week, you decide it would be excellent to add a nice, relaxing stroll to your daily routine.

You start off small, just a five minute saunter round the block, then work it up to a good couple of miles. How far can you be walking by the end of the month? Now try it wearing a snorkel. And a Princess Diana mask. Some taramasalata. Inflatable arm-bands. A bassoon. Three blind orphans. Kent. Next week, you very much expect to decide it would be an excellent idea to stop doing any more walking than is absolutely necessary.

Pisces: Your computer made entirely out of pickled onions is poorly-received in the board meeting, but delicious with small cubes of cheese. Never mind. These are the same idiots who laughed at your iPhone made entirely out of mackerel. Third time lucky. Third time: SEX TOYS MADE FROM BEEF!

~

Put your mind-hands in the air. One time. Reeeeespec' is due. Astral posse in de house!

Astral POSSEEEE!

Astral posse?

I seem to have lost the astral posse.

Well, that's inconvenient.

Let yourself out, will you? I'm going to try to lure them out with some ketamine.

39

The week of September the 24th

This week requires little introduction. Your very presence was foretold in some book, written by a chap. Go on, look all starry and impressed and read the fucking wisdom, we're all busy round here. Chop chop.

~

Aries: This week, while visiting a TV production studio built on an abandoned Cherokee graveyard, you are molested by the reanimated corpse of Jeremy Beadle. Of course, being who he is, there's that awkward couple of minutes while you wait for him to pull off the false beard and the camera crew reveals itself and everything, but nope, there you are getting your face bitten by a Beadle-Zombie. Hell of a way to go.

Taurus: You invent the concept of ringtones for genitals, but during a horrific accident, you somehow assign 'Gangnam Style' to your own private regions. Every time they are unleashed, they suddenly start pounding out the K-Pop and thrusting wildly. This actually goes down without incident and proves to be a useful ice-breaker at parties.

Gemini: One day soon, you will get lost in a library. You will wander its shelves and aisles endlessly, drinking in the wonder of encoded human creation, reminiscing about the books you read in your childhood. Listening in awe as the authors seem to drift from the pages of their creations, imploring you to take their children home, to soak in their stories and let them breath once more through your life. Or, more accurately, "you get stoned in a library".

Cancer: Celery. Once cold, hard enemy of stubborn green ennui. Now, rigid ally, bringer of crunchy sustenance. Friend of peanut butter, acquaintance of raisins. Vibrant batons of celery wave back and forth beyond your vision. "Buy us", they sing. Come on. Celery. Do it. Part of your five a day, probably. CELERY! Oh, fuck it: cigarettes it is. Meh.

Leo: The karmic wheels turn quickly for you this week, Leo. Recent evils will be revisited upon you faster than you feared, but also, good deeds. As you dealt out beatings unto clowns, so shall ye be ambushed by them and given a slap. As ye were gentle to a midget, so shall he be too, when, this week, he is the giver and you meekly receive. Next time, go to the party when the circus LEAVES, not when it arrives.

Virgo: Spiders be upon you, holy Virgo! Yes indeed, this is truly a blessed week as the heavens will shower you with nature's most beloved child: hundreds of spiders. Not just small ones, either (though you will find your share of these, too, gently caressing your nipples as you sleep) but around Wednesday, you will be utterly enraptured as a FIVE STONE TARANTULA leaps from the heavens (or a tree) and leaves a dent in the front of your Ford Cortina. Praise be for spiders! Christ, I feel itchy just writing this. Hopefully you REALLY like spiders.

Libra: Finances! Cider may be delicious and heaven knows you've worked hard, but it does look rather like you're spending upwards of 80% of your income on cider. Have you considered the healing benefits of gin?

Scorpio: A particularly bleak handful of days await you. Not only are you cornered by gypsies, barely escaping with your trousers, but that bloody public menace Enya steals your car keys and hides them in a dog. Of course, the dog is inevitably owned by - you guessed it - gyp... wait, no, actually, it's Cher. Well, that was an unexpected turn. Perhaps you should be kinder about her music in future. Watch out for tramps.

Sagittarius: The stars are hazy about your fortunes this week. Something something, 'apricots', something something 'Swiss bonds, now is the critical moment', something something 'time machine', something something 'flee to Belgium'. It's no good, I'll have to call you back.

Capricorn: An old friend of the family surprises you this week by revealing that you are secretly the last descendent of a noble race of Elves. Your true Elven name is Spanglepants Treefondler and you are called to return to your nation and ascend the throne to grasp your ancient destiny, as it is written. You do this. Remarkably, everything is fine. Your majesty.

Aquarius: This is the week where love should truly preoccupy you, Aquarius. The alignments in the heavens are now optimal for you to find The One, the single absolutely perfect, beautiful porn film that you will treasure for the rest of your life. Go now, to the dirty film shop. Tell them Barry sent you.

Pisces: Well, as you might imagine, you're mostly going to be contending with lasers this week. Between your work (with lasers), your quiet moments of relaxation (with lasers) and those thoughtful times when you look out of your window and think "Fuck me, I've got a lot of lasers", remember to take stock, to sit down and count your blessings. In this case, the BLESSINGS 4000, ULTIMATE LASER THEATRE. Of which you have five. FUCKING LASERS! WHOOOOOOOOOO! Lasers.

~

The stars do a thing, something celestial happens (probably good, if a little portentous) there's a flash of whatever, then the things recedes.

Remember: All of this is absolutely true. Doubting the wisdom of those lads is tantamount to invoking the very wrath of, you know. Stuff.

40

The week of October the 1st

Grab hold of something sturdy, you marvellous people. "Oh, no, it isn't... is it?"

Oh yes, it bloody well is. FEAST NOW UPON YOUR HORRORSCOPES!

~

Aries: Those of Ariesian nature are always drawn to walk the path less chosen. To frequent the spaces spurned by others. To loiter in the backwaters and alleyways of the soul, quietly observing, considering their schemes. Waiting. Watching. Hanging around really rather a bit too long, if we're honest. Taking photographs. Wanking, half the time. Aries are the perverts of the zodiac, this is what we're saying.

Taurus: You will be approached on the street by a young cockney urchin, attempting to sell you broccoli. The broccoli doesn't seem anything special at first glance, but you are taken by the urchin's pleading demeanour and obvious rickets, so you purchase a punnet. Upon cooking it, HEAVENS BE PRAISED! This is the ENCHANTED BROCCOLI of BETHNAL GREEN! It is talked about in pubs from Hackney lo, unto Daltson! As you bear it aloft to examine its delicate fronds in the sunlight, you brace yourself for its majesty and open your expectant eyes... It does nothing.

Gemini: You've been having the dream again. The one where you go on Dragon's Den and are trying to sell them something, then you realise that you're entirely naked. Worse yet, you're starting to find Deborah Meaden's prurient gaze arousing and it's really interrupting your presentation. Three of the Dragons immediately reject your proposal for a kind of solar-powered almond, but despite this, Duncan Bannatyne says he's in, for a 50% cut of your company, on the provision that you give him a ruddy good seeing to with a fist full of almonds.

Cancer: The moons of Jupiter are in ascendency this month, reaching their zenith on... wait... that's no MOON! That's the DEATHSTAR! You meet a tall, dark Ewok. If you do go to bed with anybody, check they're not your sister. Your power animal is: Salacious B Crumb.

Leo: Beware gypsies on jet-skis. At first it's all whooshing, splashing and lucky heather, then later, it's capsizing and curses and doing a magical wee in your begonias after midnight. Keep 'em peeled.

Virgo: Your village is a sleepy place, with little to talk of, most days. Until TODAY! Now, I know, after an intro like that, you're just sat there gagging to know what's going to happen! I know, right?! But no. The stars ain't tellin'. Nuh-uh. OK, look, between you and me, I think the stars are being dicks, so all I'm going to say is that the big thing rhymes with... um... no, I mean, it begins with 'bo'. No, that's not going to work.

Look, just keep an eye out for 'Bovril'. The secret is Bovril. You didn't hear that from me. And if you don't like being smeared with Bovril and humped by an ape, stay home. I've said too much.

Libra: Self-indulgently, you join the recent craze for onesies. After zipping yourself up in the soft, warm snugness and reflecting on how looking like a tool is a small price to play for such luxury, you realise... nobody can see you! Can it be? Yes! You were sold the famous Chameleon Onesie of Zanthar! Imbued with a magical ability to mimic the colours in its surroundings, it is said this garment was made by an ancient assassin and used to depose kings in precise, surgical hits. You mostly wear it while drinking lager and watching Sex in the City.

Scorpio: This week will see you accidentally wandering into London's first Nude Gregg's. The shop is largely as you'd imagine - staffed by a mixture of rotund, jovial folks with less than a full deck of GCSEs and horrifyingly gorgeous Polish supermodels working to send money home. The only difference here is that to get served, you have to be entirely nude. All in all, the experience is not unpleasant, but you feel they could consider handing out bibs for the gents - getting crumbs in your chest-hair is no laughing matter.

Sagittarius: A hum-drum sequence of days has left you listless and dulled by life's tedium. You must re-invigorate yourself! The stars present you with four options: 1) Learn the sitar. 2) Electronic nipple-torture. 3) Move to Kent. 4) Wolf buggery. There are no further options. CHOOSE NOW.

Capricorn: It is a well known fact that when you give love and respect to a Capricorn, they return it in kind. What is less well known is that if you give turnips and Chinese burns to a Capricorn, they wait until you're out of town, then brutally pleasure your grandma.

Aquarius: It's likely that imminently, you'll be looking for the services of a priest, owing to the somewhat truculent demons recently discovered in your underwear. This is what you get for cracking one off while consulting the ouija board. While sexting with the deceased may seem like a no-risk way to get some undead kinky jollies, you're going to be forced to handle the consequences, now that your balls are haunted.

Pisces: Lately, it has been exceedingly tempting to take up the offer of the pixie king and fly away in his magic carriage to the land of Cheam to dine upon marzipan, drink surprising wines and watch the goblins play in the forest. He sends his minions to your bedside at night to sing gentle songs of promise and seduction, leaving you to awaken with the name 'Cheam' on your lips each day. Perhaps, one day, you will finally accept this offer, never to be seen again. Mmmm. Cheam.

∼

Elucidated, titillated and spiritually sated? Fine and good!

Then get out there, my beauties! Time to grab life by the suspenders and give them a twang!

Week of October the 8th

Welcome back, friendssss. Today, we're responding to a lot of letters we've been receiving lately from your dimension and it seems as though we may have targeted the wrong species for some considerable time. So, to make amends, here are thissssss weeksssss horrorsssssscopessssss!

~

Aries: Give your owner a scare by sneaking out of your living habitat in the night and stretching out next to them while they sleep. Humans have a myth about snakes doing this to 'measure' the size of their prey, prior to consuming them. Fools. Once they're good and wound up, use their credit cards to spend a fortune on reckless internet gambling. Hahahah!

Taurus: Travel features heavily in your life recently and, just bloody typical, you're destined for a long journey next to one of those spoons who listen to dance music on awful headphones. Being a rattlesnake, you could always treat them to several hours of your own accompaniment to Justin Bieber's latest emission - ca-chicka-chick-ca-chicka-chick - or simply spit venom in his eyes, then slowly digest him, face-first, over a period of weeks. You choose the latter.

Gemini: The stars say that this week, you will meet a tall, dark mongoose. When he asks to take you out to lunch, make an excuse and LEG IT. Well, OK, no, but you know what I mean.

Cancer: Money troubles are on the horizon. It's entirely reasonable that you've been so distracted about your finances this week. What with your credit cards, long-term loans, bills, rent and pension contributions it's a wonder you haven't gone into full melt-down! NOT REALLY. YOU ARE A SNAKE! PUT DOWN THAT DEBIT CARD AND GO AND BITE SOME PEOPLE, YOU IDIOT. Jesus Christ.

Leo: You're long over-due a little YOU time, Leo. Why not call up the missus (using a complex series of hisses and pheromone secretions), grab yourself a box of hot, salted field-mouse and settle in for an evening watching a horror movie? At the cinema right now, there's that BERNARD 3D movie - the tale of a 1000ft tall human 'Bernard' which goes on the rampage, slaughtering loads of scantily-clad female snakes. Also available in infra-red.

Virgo: Life is extremely complicated at the zoo this week. Last week, there was that article about how a King Cobra has enough venom to kill an elephant. Then, earlier this week, you went and got drunk with the hyenas again and let one of them goad you into saying you could 'take on that dumb grey bastard any day'. That wasn't so good. And now? Well, it's certainly going to stir things up when Babar finds out that the real reason behind all the posturing and bad-mouthing is because all this time, you've been sleeping with his wife. Tricky situation. Tricky situation at best.

Libra: Al Wilson sings a song about you. It starts off sounding pretty groovy, a nice little melody and a song about a fine young snake getting some. But then, just as always, the inevitable snakism creeps in: the lead character's biting some poor woman and she's going to die all because of the big, bad, lying snake. You really have had enough of this sort of thing. Find Al Wilson and kill the bastard (a bite in the face will do it nicely), then lie about it.

Scorpio: Health is going to be your major worry over the next few days, as the stars report you are likely to injure yourself quite badly when, during some DIY improvements to your house, you become tangled and in a fit of extreme irony, fall down a tall ladder. The resultant attempts at humour from doctors, nurses and patients during your subsequent hospital stay leads to a total of 423 people being bitten in the face.

Sagittarius: Salman Rushdie's been on the telly again, giving it all that about morality and surprise, surprise, guess who's made out to be the big twat again? Snakes. Has he written an allegory about why badgers are fuckwits? No. Has he penned a play about some otters smoking crack? No. Voles blamed for increasingly destabilised local communities? Bollocks. He's on about the snakes again, like he always is. You bite him in the face.

Capricorn: Another freezing cold week - damn this crazy island! You're really starting to regret the decision to move to Bradford. I mean: on one hand, lovely people, thriving snake social scene, good curry. On the other, you are basically ectothermic. Perhaps it's finally time to pack up and move yourself off to the South of France to spend your retirement biting French people in the face.

Aquarius: Good news in the realms of employment! Your agent's been on the phone: a nice-sounding gentleman from a local Jewish business would like to employ you in a sales role for a very well-known fruit-named company (if you know what I mean!) I know what it sounds like, but it's not cold-calling, you'll be working with a young couple who have already expressed an interest in the product, giving them all the information they need to convince them while firmly motivating them to close the sale. Don't take 'no' for an answer! If they *do* say 'no', well, maybe just a gentle nibble on their faces to help them concentrate?

Pisces: Lately, the local human kid has become a real pain in the arse and, you know, for a snake, that's saying something. You suspect very much that it comes down to the time he's been spending with the talking bear. Speaking of which, the bear himself has been going through some really weird phases recently. Dressing himself up with fruit and flirting with monkeys. You know it's none of your business and really don't want to offend him regardless, but are starting to suspect he has some deeply-ingrained, unresolved species/gender issues. Don't feel bad about yourself if, after a long week of attempted hypnotherapy, your patience runs out - it happens to the best of people. Sometimes, the most positive way to relax is to just bite them all in the face.

~

Excsssssseellent, we ssssseeem to have got the messsssage acrosssss in the end.

Don't feel bad if a few of those tall, hairy thingsss looked a little clossssely into the eyessss of their coiled companionsss. If they didn't want biting, why would their facesss be ssssso deliciousssss? Well, quite.

Slide on, my slippery friendsssssss...

42

The week of October the 15th

Welcome, welcome, children, to the joyeous congregation of the First National Church of Skrillex the Redeemer.

Please, place your hands upon the turntables in genuflection and accept the wub into your heart.

~

Aries: A troubling week for you. While attempting to mash up the Coronation Street theme with Machine Gun by 16bit, you accidentally sprain your irony gland and end up inadvertently becoming 45 years old and really into folk music. It takes several months of therapy to wean you off corduroy and get you back on the sick breaks. In future, be careful not to attempt dangerous mashups without first googling to see if somebody has already done it and put it on YouTube. Your power animal is: The Brown Note.

Taurus: Excellent times! These last few gigs have been superb! The punters love you and you haven't dropped a bollock on the dancefloor in months. Truly, Skrillex must be proud of your diligence in filth and your collection of ridiculous trousers. Remember to observe the Sabbath; to keep it well massive. Your power animal is: A completely unexpected 70s guitar solo.

Gemini: Love is complicated for you, Gemini. You feel you may have truly connected with somebody who shares almost every aspect of your life. Your two souls soar together, entwined in a unity and bliss that you had not previously thought possible. But despite all of this, you are starting to think that she was only pretending to like that Kanji Kinetic track you put on last week and was actually quite disrespectful about Datsik. Patience may be the best path. Perhaps she was just coming down. Your power animal is: A completely unnecessary rewind.

Cancer: Finances are on your mind. While your income is reasonable, there are far too many sick tunes that must be purchased for you to get through the week without some sort of compromise. Skrill smiles upon you beatifically and suggests that you spend it all on fat slabs of wub, for as it is written, "Better to exist on cuppa soups and crackers with an iPod full of sick choons, than to grow fat listening to Jedward". Your power animal is: The 909.

Leo: BWARRRB BRWAAAAARB CHUGGA CHUGGA WIDDLY WHEEEE WHEE WWHEEEEEEE BWAAAAAAAARRB RUGGUDARUGGUDA RUGGROOOROOROOROOROO BOINK! Tinkly tinkly tinkly tinkly... plop. The new Benga CD is extremely challenging to get into a set. Your power animal is: Obscure manga samples.

Virgo: Oh, what's the point? You spend all night working your arse off, slapping on choon after choon... riding the fader, chopping that shit up, dialling up the energy and punching them in the face with the drop. All to nothing. Try some old chip-step numbers: nothing. Veer dangerously toward drum and bass for half an hour? Nothing. The last hour, you've just played Skrillex's 'Reptile' (from the Mortal Kombat movie) on repeat THIRTEEN times and literally nobody has put their hands in the air. This Christening is shit. Your power animal is: Blatant mid-track tempo-change.

Libra: Dark dreams haunt you. Music from that X-Factor show leaks into your subconscious. At work, one of your colleagues catches you whistling that fucking track by Gotye about falling out with a bird. How can this be? What could have caused you to fall so far from Skrillex's grace and majesty that he would allow these alien melodies to harangue you so? Look into your soul - have you been guilty of doubting his holy name? Ah, yes. There was that time at that party when you mentioned that frankly, you thought "Scary Monsters and Nice Sprites" was rather overrated and you were more keen on his remix work, wasn't there? Skrillex's judgement is upon you. Err not, lest he make you start enjoying Mumford and Sons. Your power animal is: Noisia remixing basically anything.

Scorpio: Diplomacy is on the menu this week. Having destroyed much of the adjoining wall shared between your house and that of your neighbours, you have considerable explaining to do. Few people truly appreciate the genius off attempting to use the theme music off of Bagpuss to underpin reversed samples of David Cameron, slathered with hypersaws and the sound of a farting woodpecker. Burying the speaker under three gallons of blancmange to get that wet, flappy sound to the sub-bass will have to wait until you've rebuilt the kitchen. Ho hum. Your power animal is: Gurning.

Sagittarius: There is a time and place for walking down the road, shouting "I AM LORD BASSINGTON, KING OF THE OSCILLATORS AND YOUR TROUSERS WILL BILLOW BEFORE ME, PEASANT!" - and 5am, outside of Gregg's the Bakers, Cheltenham high street seems as good as any other, to be perfectly honest. Haven't they been out all night, too? It's Friday for fuck's sake. Pfft. Fuck 'em! WaaAAAAaaarb wubwubwubwub. Have it, you bell-ends. Your power animal is: The filter sweep.

Capricorn: Wrexham Council are on the phone and want to talk to you about noise levels. They've just been informed about that track you dropped half an hour ago, when you set up a humungous standing bass-wave which caused everybody to immediately shit themselves. They're not angry, they thought it was hilarious and are requesting a rewind. Your power animal is: Some goths that came to the wrong club by mistake.

Aquarius: Since setting your ringtone to a random medley of powerful, bass-driven, stonking-bastard-hard tracks, you've been distinctly unimpressed with the complete lack of subsonic representation from your phone's speakers. It's almost as if they weren't designed for inaudibly low frequencies, which is ridiculous. You rectify the situation by carrying with you at all times a pair of 20" Wharfedale drivers and a generator-powered amplifier on a small cart that you call "the Bass Barrow". This solution has absolutely no drawbacks. You put some flouro lighting underneath the Bass Barrow for night-time travel. Skrillex smiles upon you. Your power animal is: Tinnitus.

Pisces: Ah, lonely, wandering Pisces. You find dubstep confusing (what is brostep? Who is Modestep? Do they really make it by recording Optimus Prime cracking one off?) - your path walks far from the footsteps of Skrillex and you have not been to confession in weeks (you know, confession, that new night in Soho, underneath the gay bar with the poster of a hippo). Be not afraid, oh yeah of gentle heart, for the waveforms of dubstep resonate inside us all. Maybe start with some Chase and Status, then work your way up from there. Your power animal is: Ending the set by playing Bananarama.

~

Wub thy brother, dear friends, and deal unto others as you would have them deal unto you.

Yo, Skrill, drop that shit like a hand-grenade. Amen.

43

The week of October the 22nd

SKRAAAA! GELFLING, YES?? LOOK AT IT, THE HORRIBLE GELFLING, COME TO DE-STROY US, YESSS??

Oh. Oh, ok. It's you, Kev. Come on in. Park your glutes, I'll put the tea on.

~

Aries: You find yourself possessed by the spirits of the dancers from Breakdance II (Electric Boogaloo). This causes all manner of involuntary body-popping throughout your week and while impressive in terms of athleticism and rhythm, it's beginning to make your job as an undertaker extremely difficult. You pull off a really difficult head-spin on top of an urn and literally nobody in the procession will give you some skin. Your power animal is: Chaka Khan.

Taurus: A pelican makes off with your wrist-watch! You chase the blighter down the street until it becomes apparent that you have travelled through time and are now wandering around 1940s Kent. This is no problem! You immediately deploy your turn-of-the-century Kent Businessman disguise and are soon accepted into the local society. Disaster strikes when the pelican is revealed to be none other than... PROFESSOR MORIARTY! That conniving master-criminal has somehow engineered your demise across time and space! You have a quick word with him and suspiciously, it all turns out to be completely fine. Weird! Your power animal is: the Flux Capacitor

Gemini: It's not easy being a Constructicon and the stars know that things aren't likely to be any different for you over the next few days. Half the time, you're shovelling dirt and digging foundations for (evil) storage facilities, then suddenly you're walking around, expected to engage Autobots in armed combat and wise-crack about their inferior capabilities. Then, to add insult to injury, just when you think you can sit down and have some 'me time', you're expected to combine with four of your colleagues to form DEVASTATOR. You really can't get any peace. Plus, you've been comfort-eating and all those energon calories are really starting to go to your thighs. Ho hum. Your power animal is: Luton Airport (which converts into a massive laser cannon).

Cancer: Love beckons this week! That's right, brace yourself for a news-flash as this week, a whirlwind of romance enters your life as, on a business trip to Wales, you find yourself falling head-over-heels in love with the charming market town of Aberystwyth! Beware, though, as despite its promises, you soon come to believe your darling Aber might be batting its eyelashes at nearby Shrewsbury. The whore. Your power animal is: frustration.

Leo: Enough! To hell with reason, arm yourself to the

teeth and go postal! The doorbell rings and it's some dick selling you home insurance? Waste the fucker! You get to work and the secretary bitches about you being late? Smoke that mother! The boss wants to talk to you? HELL YEAH! YOU KINDA WANT TO TALK TO HIM, TOO! You storm in there, kick the door down and as the smoke starts to clear, growl the words you were born to utter: COMPLIMENTARY ANAL BEADS! On reflection, this didn't play out the way you'd imagined. Your power animal is: GIN.

Virgo: Your body aches, life is one never-ending hang-over. Your clothes can stand up on their own and sufficient items in your fridge have achieved sentience as to make you responsible for genocide when you finally remembered to plug it back in. You are currently eating peanut butter out of a wok, using a Jacob's cream cracker. Basically, everything is going according to plan. Your power animal is: some bees covered in marmalade.

Libra: Don your turnip helmet, for today, you are VEGETABLOR, THE GREEN AVENGER! All will fall before your mighty battle-leeks and weep. Your power animal is: David Cameron.

Scorpio: In your next life, you visit a hypnotist to find out information about your previous life. He will get you to remember back over thoughts of your life, until your birth, then keep going, back into the life before, the moments before death, every minute, every second, all you see and hear. You're just getting to the bit where you read this line. This is that, NOW. That hypnotist is fucking GOOD. When you wake up, you'll be in the future, but it will be the now to you, then.

Your power animal is: lap-dancers.

Sagittarius: You keep having that dream again, lately. The one where you go to work, completely clothed. You wake up feeling sick, but sort of aroused. Your power animal is: the tetrahedron.

Capricorn: Finances are on your mind. Particularly, you notice that every time you spend more than £10 on your credit card, you wake up to find a small, ripe, delicious plum placed next to your bed. It doesn't matter where you are, or if you sleep alone or surrounded by cameras it's always the same. You've tried transferring money to your debit card and spending on that instead: no plums. You've taken out £9.99, then 1p: no plums. £10 or more, there's always a plum. On holiday in Spain, you spend €11.77 and there it is. The plum. You have no idea how they find you or what motivates them to do this... or who THEY are, and where they get such delicious plums. Deep in their underground lair, they watch you on tiny monitors and peer through your expenses on glowing green terminals. Smiling. Waiting. Biding their plums. Your power animal is: financially-linked plum-receipt.

Aquarius: Now, of all times, is a bad moment to suddenly reveal your prejudice toward midgets. Just swallow, pay the little feller, pull on your jeans and let's get the fuck out of here. Your power animal is: Basingstoke.

Pisces: On passing through a local cyber-gypsy commune, you decide to get your elbows fitted with USB ports. This is hugely convenient for recharging your phone, but a little annoying when your friends keep asking if they can borrow your elbow when their iPad runs out of charge at the coffee shop. Inevitably, somebody at work decides to one-up you and gets Thunderbolt connectors installed in their nipples. Your power animal is: a discreetly-placed PCMCIA socket.

∿

Glad we got the whole "Gelfling" mixup out of the way there. Sorry about that. Old habit, you see, my mom's half-Skeksis, and you know what it's like.

Anyway, be lucky.

44

The week of October the 29th

Close the door, silently, brother. It seems the last of our number has arrived. Put your feet up and give your kimono a rest as we intone the sacred wisdom of NINJA HORRORSCOPES!

~

Aries: This could be a difficult week. While scaling a vertical castle wall to assassinate a powerful land-owner, your mobile phone somehow gets pressed and you end up butt-dialling your girlfriend. She hears a few minutes of breathing and grunting, then somebody shrieking while you yell "NOW YOU FEEL MY WRATH!" - She immediately assumes that you're balls-deep in the barmaid. When talking doesn't solve things and you become tired of dodging thrown kitchen-ware, you reluctantly deploy smoke pellets and disappear into the night like a shadow.

Taurus: You meet a tall, dark stranger beneath a silvery moon. In accordance with your training, you immediately execute a spinning leg-sweep, then a high cutting blow to the larynx before finishing them with your Sai. In this instance, it turns out to be a courier bearing something you bought from Amazon. You deploy smoke pellets and disappear into the night like a shadow.

Gemini: This is a good week for your finances. Neptune dominates the skies, ensuring the flow of gold into your pockets as local warlords pursue their blood-debts. Your clan is in high demand and you double your profits by fighting for both sides. Tuesday is marred briefly when, due to administrative cock-up, you accidentally end up in a vicious rooftop sword battle with your own nan. Well, one ninja does very much look like another, especially at night. An unexpectedly slippy tile prevents accidental nanicide - as the silly old mare tumbles off the roof, you take the opportunity to deploy smoke pellets and make a like shepherd.

Cancer: Consider the crab you are named for, Cancer-san. He hugs his body low to the ground, keeps his eyes upon the subject of his hunger and moves sideways, never directly forward. Like a crab, you must become hard on the outside, yet remain delicious on the inside and good with a lightly salted salad. Consider the crab. The CRAB. The stars say you have crabs. Deploy smoke pellets now.

Leo: Decisions, decisions. Lower ventrical, neat (if powerful) burst over the painting, or in underneath the ribs and pull the whole kaboodle out and to hell with the priceless rug? You've heard about porn magazine editors that become so inured to their work that they spend most of their time agonizing over the interior decoration behind the shot than the myriad wangs and their improbable destinations. Now it seems you're more concerned with protecting works of art than turning your enemies into walking sashimi. Perhaps it's time to get into porn. Do ninjas do porn? You deploy smoke pellets and are ruminating so deeply you almost forget to disappear.

Virgo: Some days, you wonder if you should ever have abandoned your dreams of opening a barbecue-chicken restaurant on the Champs-Élysées. Making a silent, internal decision, you deploy your smoked poulets and disparaissez.

Libra: Hubris, venerable Libra... hubris! You are so busy laughing at the sight of another stupid samurai falling upon their sword on the battle-field that you slip on some entrails and fall on your keys. Oh, sweet-and-sour pork, that's a bastard. Disappearing is out of the question, so you glide mysteriously sideways, clutching at an area between your leg and your balls.

Scorpio: Ah, you seek the next challenge, do you, unenlightened one? After many years of working in the night, at one with the shadows, you seek greater meaning? Then yes. You have achieved a great victory in the inner battle all must face and you have earned this advice: Search out the temple of the Golden Wonder. Once you defeat the guard and make your way inside, fill your pack with the ultimate reward - the SPICY TOMATO WHEAT CRUNCHIES. They will see you well through a truly massive hangover. If you can't find them, get your laughing gear around some Nice and Spicy Nik Naks. Deploy your smokey-bacon Wotsits and disappear.

Sagittarius: It is a strange week. Your master, Shredder, has pitted you and your brothers against what he claims is your greatest threat to obtaining a foothold in the valuable and lucrative criminal underworld of New York. In a showdown planned for months, your forces are finally unleashed and you face: four teenage mutant turtles. You're told they're ninja, but really, they look like cos-players. Well, they look like cos-players for about 30 seconds, then they start to resemble something very much like lasagne. You feel sort of guilty about this, particularly if they were just teenagers. This is about one step away from crashing a kids birthday party, stabbing them up and nicking the cake. You deploy slightly more smoke pellets than usual to avoid looking your brethren in the eye as you disappear.

Capricorn: Concentrate! Be ever alert and give your all to your path, lest the spirits of the elders seek to tutor you! A few moments of self-indulgence are really going to come back to bite you this week as your clan brothers, sick of hearing you complain about the state of your barnet, have secretly paid the sensei's munting daughter to dress up as your missus and take you down a peg or two. As the old saying goes, the whingey ninja with the ginger fringe that makes him cringe misses the minge and fingers the minger.

Aquarius: Another day on the Ninj. You've been ninjing it up good and proper lately, but somebody always wants to take down a good, honest evil mercenary killer-for-hire who trades in indiscriminate, clandestine slaughter. Bruce Lee. Chuck Norris. PIRATES. Drunken singers from promising local industrial bands inexplicably hunting ninja in music venues in northern fishing villages. You thought you had met and fought them all, until today, screaming from the skies came that infernal Irish bint, gabbling about whales and Robin Hood. ENYA. Which she just explained at considerable length is some kind of fucking Irish acronym for ENemY to all ninjA. Then she drank all your saké and did a wee on your best ceremonial rug. She is fucking insane. If you see her again, you're going to rip her nipples off.

Pisces: Dreams have been chasing around your mind, where only thoughts of silent destruction should dwell. Can a ninja be dissolved by vinegar? Was Belinda Carlisle the first true ninja? Does it make you MORE ninja to do your ninjing while listening to the Wu-Tang Clan? Is it true that ninjas cannot surf? Can ninjas become zombies? Does that make them slow, obvious ninja (lame) or quick, invisible zombies (Shit!) What about ninja with tentacles? Could Uhuru plus a Zulu create Cthulujutsu? Or is it just you? You should possibly not be swallowing your smoke pellets, little ninja, they will make your mind disappear.

~

Let yourself out, brother, for the night curls arounds us and... oh right, you all just fucked off, did you? I see.

I'll close up then, shall, I? Charming.

45

The week of November the 5th

Greetings, haggard-one. You must have travelled hard and long in the storm for your face speaks volumes of your troubles. I mean, seriously. Jesus. Have you considered moisturising?

~

Aries: The stars think you need more greens in your diet, Aries. You're not looking after yourself. Doesn't have to be vegetables! Oh, god, no. Steak... dumplings... dolly mixtures... Big Mac... lard... anything really. Just paint it green and down the hatch. Delicious.

Taurus: After the initial warning about going 'commando' at work, you are now resigned to wearing underwear each and every day. Anything to keep those prudes off your back. You'll note, however, that they didn't specify WHERE you had to wear the undergarments. Pants on your elbows and balls swaying freely in the breeze it is, then! (The stars acknowledge that the reader may not own balls per se, but credits them with sufficient intelligence as to take the hint).

Gemini: For the rest of the week, you are instructed to answer only to the name "Nipples McKlusky". Anyone who addresses you in any other way is to be summarily pressed to your chest while you reiterate "I SAID. MY NAME. IS NIPPLES. MCKLUSKY". You will go far with this advice.

Cancer: You are recruited to form a covers band for 80s Ska-pop sensation Amazulu. After three somewhat haphazardly-promoted gigs in the heart of Surrey, you step onto the stage to be confronted by your old nemesis: ENYA. Frankly, you can't help but think she's really crossed a line this time by blacking up.

Leo: After many years of suffering and building your plans, you finally reveal to the world your alter-ego, the hero nurtured inside, beneath the veneer of normality. You are... TIKITIS! THE SILENT AVENGER! Blessed with the power (a lead pipe) to combat the forces of evil (people playing music too loudly on public transport)! You spend the next two years soundly beating strangers on the London Underground for listening to iPods or playing music out of their phone speakers. Eventually, you are caught by the police, who thank you and give you a delicious pie.

Virgo: While stoned and staring into a poster of a fractal in the eye of a visiting alien (who is, himself, smoking a joint), you are overtaken by a deep sense of calm and understanding. Immediately, the meaning of life is apparent to you in its simple, perfect form. In one single word, you have the answer. THE answer. That word is 'BISCUITS'.

Libra: You're not sure how this spree really began

but here you are, in the middle of the town centre, covered in mackerel, punching a monk. You didn't even know there were any monks in Leeds. You stop, briefly, and the monk looks up at you as you stand still, about to speak, as though you might somehow explain the violence (and fish) you have rained down upon him. But no. The moment passes and you figure you might as well get on with the task at hand. Otherwise how will you explain all the mackerel? Exactly.

Scorpio: Each new person you meet from now on must be tasted. Lick their faces thoroughly, trying to leave as even a covering of saliva as possible. When you are finished, write extensive notes about each tasting in your leather-bound Book of Friends. This is perfectly normal. Do as we say.

Sagittarius: Ah, Sagittarius. With your face like a walnut's scrotum.

Capricorn: Learn the harmonica. When life gets you down and you're all alone, you will always have the harmonica. You will always have music for your soul, and music is a better friend than any man or woman could be. You may also want to stock up on porn. And gin.

Aquarius: The first person you see after reading this message will be your beloved for the rest of your life. The second is your mortal enemy: strike them down at the first opportunity before they poison this Earth further. The third person you meet after reading this message, ah. That person, dear reader, that person is Bernard. Run up to them, give 'em a knowing wink and say 'HEY HEY, BERNARD!' Regardless of how they react, you will know you have done a fine deed. A Bernard never forgets.

Pisces: This week is the perfect opportunity to re-connect with nature. You must spend time among the fields and meadows, breathing deeply and taking in the beauty and majesty of the Earth. Converse with the noble otter in his den. Whisper to the wise old owl. Get drunk with Old Man Stoat and his kin. Take PCP with some badgers and rob a bank, lightly-wounding three security guards and leading to a five year custodial sentence. Okay, you have now connected too closely with nature. Back off. Back off. Baaaaack off. There we go.

~

The time of the unburdening is done. Put on your hat and face the world, traveller. There are biscuits. And there is gin.

46

The week of November the 12th

Quick, friends! Climb aboard your shining Kawasaki motorbikes of TRUTH and let us chase the car of justice beyond the roundabout of doubt and into the motorway of stretched metaphor! Let us seek out our HORRORSCOPES!

~

Aries: Everybody on the train with glasses is looking at you. Oh yes, they are. And they can all hear your thoughts. Oh yes. They're listening. There's only one way to block it all out. Go on. Stand up, drop your trousers and scream CHEESE CHEESE CHEESE CHEESE! Do it now, before it's too late.

Taurus: In olden times, one way to divine the unknowable will of the gods was to cast yarrow stalks and interpret the way they fell by reading the ideograms of the I Ching. Nowadays, we have technology where once blind faith led the way - no more I Ching, only iPhones. In the same way, however, these modern gadgets can help us to work sense from the mystery of the universe. See if you can collect six iPhones together, then throw them at the floor as hard as you can. Much wisdom will befall you.

Gemini: Oh, gods, there's nothing to be done with you this week. You are infested with mind-worms. Only gin can cure you. As your doctor and/or priest, I insist you take the day off and see to this vile infection. When you come back, I want you to be seeing four of me and singing about pixies. Go on. Off you fuck.

Cancer: A wise man once told you "All Belgians are prostitutes". Now you're older and wiser yourself, you still can't say for certain if he was right, but the last five you met DEFINITELY WERE.

Leo: This week will be seen through the lens of the 80s for you, Leo. And mostly in a bad way. You will forced to wear leg-warmers, made redundant and Max Headroom with punch you in the cock with a Rubik's cube while China Crisis drink your Quatro. On the up-side, you will accidentally stagger into a spontaneous street party as a bunch of cheerleaders and a bodybuilder dude with a saxophone appear from nowhere and are immediately and gratuitously topless. You're so surprised you inadvertently come on Eileen.

Virgo: Much of your attention has been focused in one place, lately. Examining the pelvis of this goose has really kept you absorbed, but now, the task is coming to an end and you have to ask yourself what will take its place? Will you examine another goose's pelvis? Will you examine something else belonging to the same goose? Perhaps you'll let the goose examine YOUR pelvis, I mean, fair's fair. Yes. Yes, that would be nice, wouldn't it? Let the goose have a look at your pelvis. Just a glimpse. It's perfectly legal.

Libra: You are hereby tasked with discovering what the fuck the point of Canada Dry was. If you suss that out, I'll give you a shiny new sixpence. And some gin.

Scorpio: When you find stress overwhelming you in your workplace, try this ancient technique: stand upright, but relaxed. Allow your shoulders to fall back slightly. Bring your hands up so that your fingertips touch just in front of your face. Repeat this mantra: "Meditation is for dicks. Meditation is for dicks. If somebody doesn't bring me a coffee and some Krispy Kremes in the next five minutes, I swear I'm going to stab a bitch. Meditation is for dicks..." - Let the anxiety just gently roll out of you and, if necessary, do stab that bitch.

Sagittarius: The weather in your emotional ecosystem has been tempestuous lately - you have found your heart blown around like a leaf in a storm, leaving you worn and tired, slow to connect to others. And that's why you're watching the movie of the dolphin being beaten up by ninjas with cricket bats, with your trousers round your ankles. No more explanation needed. Next time I'll knock before I come in. Lesson learned.

Capricorn: When shaking hands with somebody, take a moment to think of all the things they will have done with that hand, possibly even today. They might have eaten... cleaned themselves... pleasured themselves... punched a clown... pleasured a clown... scratched an itch... scratched an itchy clown. You get the picture. Just let that run through your mind at your next business lunch.

Aquarius: Yo! You! Aquarius! RIGHT NOW, BUD-DY! You need to DRINK! You need to DANCE! You need to throw back your head and shout WHEEEE HEEEEE, I'M THE FUCKING KING OF THE LIZ-ARDS, BABY, AND I DON'T NEED NO MOTHER-FUCKING HAIRCUT! - Then spin, grab whoever's nearest, kiss them and just stroll out into the night to see what the world has in store for you. GO!

Pisces: Look up into the night sky when you next have the chance. See if you can spot the brightest star of the night - you know the one. Now, look down and to the left a little, you should see a smaller, less-bright star, in a clump of three, twinkling away. That star is, in fact, a small dog. Not a star. Not a dog-star. Just a small, extremely bright dog. In space. And it's run-ning toward you veeeeeerry slowly. And when it gets down to earth, maybe while you sleep, maybe while you're reading... it's going to give you a lick. Right on the ankle. Space-dog style. (Left ankle).

~

Ride on, traveller. I must stop and consume this mug of hot Bovril at the roadside of con-templation. I may also partake of the Pickled Onion Monstermunch of introspection.

Leave me now. I have only enough for one.

47

The week of November the 19th

Ah yes, a new visitor, a new pleasure! Let us see - do you carry the sacred birthmark of the horse upon your ghostly white buttock? Hmmm. I suspect that may be Marmite if I'm not mistaken, but still, here we are. Brace yourself.

~

Aries: Life is too fast. There is no good reason for you to have to adopt this frenetic pace. Pretty much everything can be done from home, hell, from bed! Take a stand... lying down. Refuse to come into work. Deny ALL attempts to entrouser you. Order a week's worth of pizza, crack open that DVD boxed set of Friends and get your telecommute on. Pretty much the worst they can do is fire you, bankrupt you and try to evict you. By then, you should be waaaaay too big for them to get through that door. Take it easy.

Taurus: This habit of buying a load of footballs, drawing faces on them, stacking them on your sofa and having a raucous one-man-party is getting out of hand. Particularly when the lights go down and things get intimate. That's just not right. Putting lipstick on them doesn't make it better.

Gemini: Listen to one song by Chaka Khan every day this week, ideally around breakfast. It will do you untold good.

Cancer: Do you believe in angels? Well, even though the answer to that is probably 'no', you've been under the protective wing of your own private guardian angel for some time now. All the times that good luck caught up with you or bad luck passed you by... the parking ticket you didn't get, the pay-rise you did... all the work of angels. Even while you sleep, the angels are there, protecting you, watching you, taking photographs of you, smearing their nipples with Vaseline and licking you. Angels.

Leo: This is really not the ideal week for you to be caught watching an Ewok wanking Gok Wan off through the eye of a needle and into a wok. Nevertheless, this is your fate.

Virgo: When you were young, for quite a while, you felt you might be a robot, perhaps - or maybe a space alien or shade from another astral plane. Your insides never seemed to be wired up the same as everyone else, you always stuck out. This week, during a surprise visit, you walk in to discover your family without their human masks on, chittering away to each other while their tentacles gently ooze a poisonous green liquid. After the initial embarrassment, you concede that this explains a lot.

Libra: Damnit, you hate getting custard in your beard. This is doing absolutely nothing for your burgeoning glamour model career. One of these days you're going to have to shave, give up trifle and get some actual modelling contracts. One of these days.

Scorpio: Love life: You will meet a tall, dark stranger. He will yell something at you in Welsh, then proceed to administer a near-fatal bumming. It turns out he's a carpenter and you look dangerously like the chap who murdered his wife (brutally, mind). He apologises by way of carving the words "terribly sorry" into fourteen beautiful and unique wooden spoons.

Sagittarius: Over the next few days, try to steer clear of goths. This is their rutting season and it's a well-known fact that their floppy, crimped fringes and ridiculous eyebrows often cause them to accidentally initiate mating procedures with non-goths, owls, lamp-posts, etc. If you ARE a goth, just try to keep it together, will you?

Capricorn: This week you will unleash a poo so frightening, so *ridiculous*, so unfathomably dense, so mighty in girth and so tortuous to the olfactory senses that the very devil himself will appear before you in a flash of smoke and brimstone, shout "DUDE!" and slap you in the mouth. Don't be afraid. Own it.

Aquarius: After months of hunting, the goal is near. Finally, you feel in your bones that you must be drawing close to the secret, hidden lair of that fucking cow Enya and her mewling, cack-faced fiddle-players. You have travelled far, to deliver the ultimate weapon: the 1996 Scooter Ibiza Summer Season Mix Tape, which must be fired right up her auxiliary exhaust port (right below the main port). Don your hilarious vintage raving outfit and daub the Vix Vaporub into your warrior's mask. Your time will come!

Pisces: Your collection of Boglins from the last few decades turn out to be both sentient and very much alive. You are declared their queen. At least, you very much hope that's what that word meant. You can't help but think about all the times you put your hands up inside them and made their eyes bulge.

~

Remove the blindfold once more, little one, the horrors have retreated back to their home dimensions and my trousers are once again firmly buttoned. But make your retreat quickly, for the beast seldom sleeps long.

48

The week of November the 26th

Clutch your loved-ones, grit your teeth and gaze mindlessly into the maelstrom as we prepare to bring you this week's terrifying yet mellifluous HORRORSCOPES!

~

Aries: When asked, onlookers of the forthcoming massacre will generally claim to be equally horrified by the fact that the victims were strangled to death with an umbilical cord as the fact that you fervently insist 'the baby did it'.

Taurus: On opening your Kinder egg today, you discover inside it is an identical, smaller Kinder egg. Within this egg is another egg. And another. And another. Eventually, you crack open the last egg and inside, discover a perfectly detailed statuette of the pope buggering a Volvo, made from delicious vanilla fudge. Which, you concede, was a surprise.

Gemini: Love: This week, you attempt to give a friend your penultimate Rolo, but, due to a miscalculation, accidentally hand her your last one. According to the advertising legislation, you are then legally obliged to marry them. Fortunately, the ceremony is disrupted when a giant, anthropomorphic hippo in evening-wear appears and stampedes toward you, screaming blue murder because of something you told the children. Just when you think it's all settled down, you are arrested for illicit consumption of a Kia-Ora.

Cancer: Don't give up. There is always something else to try. And if you run out of ideas, there are always pictures of cats on the internet. There is always porn. There will always be gin. You can do them at the same time if it's a really bad one.

Leo: Every time you are met with somebody who is staggeringly over-opinionated and decides to share with you despite your clear indifference, try licking your lips slowly and drawling "mmmmmm. DELICIOUS. Yes." If they continue, start rubbing your nipples. If they still continue, start rubbing theirs.

Virgo: Inside every fat, flabby, sweaty, balding man is a slender, lithe young feller. Pounding away to pay the rent.

Libra: You live inside a glistening palace made of ice cubes, slowly and silently dripping, dissolving. A testament to the ephemeral nature of all beauty, reflecting, refracting, warping the mundane and accentuating the fragile power of the soul. An artistic triumph, a bold stand against the light, a temple to the transitory. No, Libra, you do not. You live in Portsmouth. Portsmouth. Say it with me, Libra. "Portsmouth".

Scorpio: The issue with having named your genitals

"The Revolution" turns out to be that while it's good fun to proclaim loudly that "The Revolution will not be televised!" you get devastatingly drunk one night and suddenly and it is. On the news. Right after Corrie. Thank god you shaved.

Sagittarius: When you look into the sky and see planes soaring through the air and wonder if they're looking back down at you, the answer is "yes". And they think you should put some clothes on, frankly. Also, you really don't want to know what the bloke who takes the pictures for Google Maps thinks about your antics.

Capricorn: Consider a pebble. Eroded by the elements. Old and worn soft, but solid and resilient. A hippy walks down a beach and picks up the beautiful old stone. He takes it back with him, to his lair, where he carefully places the pebble on a table, drills a hole through it and puts it on eBay for a tenner. Don't be a pebble. Punch a hippy.

Aquarius: Due to an administrative error, every task in your weekly plan has been replaced with "twerking". 9:30am: Twerking with the marketing department. 11:00: A presentation in which you will be twerking to staff from the production crew. After lunch, you have a 4-way conference-twerk with the Shanghai office and finally, a few hours left at the end of the day to catch up on some personal twerking on your own. Get to it.

Pisces: If you listen very carefully at night, you're sure you can hear a droning sound, quietly in the background. Quietly, but getting louder. A warming, familiar sound that reminds you of the past. A feeling of spinning, of whirring, bringing you a quiet joy. When you awaken, all thoughts of this sound will be gone and you certainly don't linger outside B&Q, looking earnestly into their window, plotting and planning. Well. Maybe just a bit.

~

Now, at last, you may relax your weary muscles, sit back in your leather Wisdom Reception Throne and drink deeply of the sachet of complimentary Post-Enlightenment Curative Broth™. Let your neurones rest a while, you won't be needing them for the rest of the day.

49

The week of December the 3rd

Baby! The camera loves you! Yeah, that's right! Come a little closer, let the lens drink you in, sugar... you're gonna look GREAT on the cover of this week's HORRORSCOPES...

~

Aries: If you're being bullied or pressurised, sometimes it can help to try to see the world through the eyes of your bully. And for that, you're going to need a ball-peen hammer and a good hiding place.

Taurus: Today, while idly relaxing and looking at clouds, you will finally realise the horrifying truth about paperclips. (Hint: that talking one is their leader).

Gemini: To combat pressure at work, consider printing the faces of your colleagues onto sticky paper, then adhering them to your naked buttocks and genitals before you dress. Throughout the working day (for instance, in a confrontational meeting that is making you feel anxious), think about your secret photographs and smile.

Cancer: Remember, revenge is best served cold. On ice, perhaps. With a little lemon. Basically, revenge is gin. Chin chin.

Leo: Cabbages, cabbages, cabbages, cabbages, cabbages, cabbages, cabbages, cabbages - YES! Beetroot, beetroot, beetroot, beetroot, beetroot, beetroot, beetroot - NO! Man, why do you have to be so harsh to the beetroot? You're pretty much being racist to a vegetable. I'm not sure I even know you any more.

Virgo: This week, the stars say that you are extraordinarily likely to wake up in the morning as the reincarnation of Vanilla Ice. This is a mixed blessing. Your ability to glow in the dark is greatly improved, as indeed is your facility for chump-waxing (particularly in the manner of a candle). However, your surname is now 'Van Winkle' and you look like a tool. Swings and roundabouts, Bob. Swings and roundabouts.

Libra: Lately, everything seems to be tasting of marzipan. Puddings... sausages... ice-cream... the car... your wife. You panic briefly and search the internet (in case, you know, 'everything tasting like marzipan' is some sort of warning sign of brain cancer or something) but no, it seems fine, just odd. I mean, it's not like marzipan tastes so bad. After a few weeks, you realise the mistake: Tesco Own Brand Marzipan Toothpaste! The plain packaging makes it practically identical to the mint stuff. By this time, however, you've got used to the flavour. Mmmm. Marzipan.

Scorpio: Don't blame the eels. They're just looking for somewhere warm to cuddle up - excitable little fellers! And don't blame that friendly Chinese geezer with the funnel, he just works here! Really, at this stage, you've only got yourself to blame. Or possibly your agent. Either way, you're going to need a bucket pretty soon. Sploosh!

Sagittarius: Hire the midgets. Unpack the stirrups. Put on the clown wig. Attach the clamps. Roll in the marmalade. Turn up the Justin Bieber. Release the bees. This is the last time anyone will ever say you're not romantic.

Capricorn: The end-times approach. You thought you had cornered that lying, caterwauling harridan Enya in her secret Leprechaun Lair, deep beneath the shrieking mountains, but when you burst through the door to her strong-hold, somehow she had already escaped. SOMEHOW she knew you were coming. One night, while he sleeps, you approach the bunk of your first in command and carefully pull at his beard. Before disbelieving eyes, his beard and entire face gently peel away to reveal... ENYA. HERE! ALL ALONG! And you'd recently started having some pretty violent sex with this guy, too. ENYAAAAAAAAAAA!

Aquarius: Love life: You meet a tall, dark, handsome Chuckle Brother. It's Barry. He looks like a shaved badger with a brush up its arse, but he makes you laugh, so you give him a whirl. It all comes crashing down when after a night on the town and a nose full of columbian marching powder, he suggests his brother pops round. In the morning, you wake up alone, tattered and torn, all you can focus on is the same four words, over and over. "To me. To you." You will never be clean again.

Pisces: The extra tentacles you will sprout this week should be no cause for alarm. You notice that, in particular, they are of great assistance in household chores and particularly DIY. While your hands are busy holding and using the drill, for instance, your tentacles can hold a sandwich, help you read a book, greet a friendly orphan, call a friend or prepare a delicious, crisp salad! Mostly, though, you use them for holding another eight drills. News reports in your area this week tend to have focussed on that, though if anything, your main objection to the phrase "drill-wielding octo-mutant" is that they aren't actually counting your total number of limbs. DUH.

~

That's a wrap, you crazy kids. You take five, now. Relax, unwind, rehydrate.

We've got to set up the cameras for the next scene. Don't let it get cold, y'hear?

50

The week of December the 10th

Welcome! Soul-searchers, future-seekers, chasers of the impossible knowledge - all are welcome here. Attend as we dispense the final, accurate, precisely unyielding truths that will define your very lives.

~

Aries: Night fever, night feverrrrrr! - CAN KILL. Avoid a hideous death from Night Fever by constantly flying around the globe, staying always within the sun's life-giving rays. Never sleep.

Taurus: There are not many Pandas left in the world. It is an unfortunate time for you to discover, now, that you find them absolutely delicious. From their silly furry faces down to their cute little toesies, they are a succulent treat and no mistake. No wonder they're nearly all gone.

Gemini: Your porn name is Rusty Fudge-Hammer. Your favourite position is The Unwelcome Sailor. Your most popular DVD appearance is as Gringo #4, scene 2 of Taco Juan For Thee Team - Mexican Love Machines volume 2. Your eventual reason for retirement: you permanently sprain it in a particularly complex scene where Enya and a man dressed as a jackdaw attempt to mount you simultaneously in the back of an aged Volvo.

Cancer: Erase the files. Burn the hard drive. Apply the moustache. Board the plane. Never look back. Nobody must ever discover that you are secretly Noel Edmonds.

Leo: After years of denial, you now accept that it is time to step out from the shadows and tell your family the truth: you are and always have been a secret lemonade drinker. You've been trying to give it up, but it's one of those nights.

Virgo: You are volatile and unreasonable when you have been drinking the night before. Also, while you are drinking. And the time prior to a drink tends to be pretty brutal, too. It may simply be that you're what scientists call a 'git'.

Libra: What if your boss was, in fact, inflatable? Imagine that. All this time, you've been taking orders from some hollow, inflatable, literal windbag! Preposterous! You shouldn't have to put up with that kind of indignity! Get a pin! You know what to do!

Scorpio: It appears the pandemic was almost laughably avoidable. If you had simply put the lid back on, millions could have been saved. Still. Never, mind. It's only Belgium.

Sagittarius: Nobody is for one minute going to believe your explanation of how you got a candelabra all the way up there.

Capricorn: Today, you will receive the call on behalf of all people - the delegations of the world have come together in one place at one time to make their will known. As one voice, the people of all mankind formally DEMAND that you stop listening to Guns and Roses. They are a bloody shambles.

Aquarius: You will be visited by a strangely familiar-looking kangaroo who reveals themselves to be your birth-mother. Nodding confusedly, you think back to your earliest memories of seeing life from a bouncing furry pocket as mom gently pats your head, pops you in and sets off back to Melbourne. Streuth!

Pisces: You think you might have got a little out of hand last week, with the drills and the tentacles and the destruction (and the indiscriminate murdering - oops!) but this week, you're doing much better and it's all under control. You're only going to drill ONE thing today, and it's going to be fine and people will thank you for it, then you will have a little rest. That thing? Coventry.

~

Again, we part. We trust the stars were generous with each of you, but remind you that if the path disclosed seems unfavourable and not to your liking, it is within each of us to manifest our own destiny, to challenge the will of the Gods, to DEFY THE VERY UNIVERSE OF

SPACE AND TIME.

Assuming, of course, that you possess the Sacred Amulet of Zanthar. Obviously. Otherwise, you're stuffed.

51

The week of December the 17th

Katanga, my cheeky little wisdom-seekers! Pin back your lug-holes and get ready for truth, it's very much time to receive your HORROR-SCOPES!

~

Aries: This week, you will discover that your underwear has, inevitably, become sentient. Your first conversations are really quite combative as they give you some home truths about the state of your undercarriage, but eventually a truce is reached. By promising to be more considerate in future, you are able to get them to agree to stop making disparaging comments every time you're about to get lucky. Further problems arise, though, when they form a strategic alliance with your genitals (also sentient).

Taurus: Ever get caught out in the rain and notice that all the people in suits are so well-organized? Those guys ALWAYS have umbrellas, damnit! Next time, try running up to them and giving them a big cuddle while you share their brolly - they're friendlier than you think!

Gemini: You really should have learned by now that caramel is delicious, but rarely a wise choice as lubricant.

Cancer: The darkness and heaviness you feel in your soul can be lifted, it is up to you. Take a deep breath, acknowledge your own inner beauty and gently remove your concrete butt-plug. Run free.

Leo: Ricky Martin visits you unexpectedly in the evening to ask why you stopped listening to "La Vida Loca". He claims not to be disappointed, but you can still tell that he thinks you let him down. You dance to salsa music into the night and eventually make sensuous love for hours on top of a mahogany bookcase. In the morning, he is gone.

Virgo: You relent to your most basic, primal urges and find yourself, late on a Sunday afternoon, pushing a goose up a tube. You feel certain this was not what you had planned for the weekend, yet here you are. Eventually, though, you start to acclimatise and embrace the goose-tube. Many happy weekends of poultry insertion lie ahead.

Libra: Police find you undeniably guilty of whistling in Oslo. You are fined 14p and given a warning. And a sherry. And a slightly awkward cuddle that lingers just a bit too long. And another sherry. And a peck on the cheek. And another sherry. Eventually, you all have sex in a cathedral. On the way home, you catch yourself whistling the theme to 'Allo allo', but it's too late, the police are already on the scene. As a second offence, the fine doubles. So does the sherry.

Scorpio: Due to an unfortunate misunderstanding with a local gypsy, your mobile telephone starts to turn into a lizard at night. This is mostly fine, as it returns to your pocket to sleep, transforming once more into a phone during the daytime (when you receive the majority of your communications) but you can't help but wonder if it's listening when you make calls. And you did take some pictures of your... you know. Yes. Hmm.

Sagittarius: You are a bum-wizard. Don't believe it? Next time you are using the bathroom, just before the main event (so to speak) try standing up, proclaiming "ABRACADABRA!" in a booming voice, then promptly sitting back down... now that's magic!

Capricorn: You have been sleeping poorly recently, which is slowly turning each day into a tired, depleted struggle. It wasn't always like this. What has changed? Look inside yourself and you will find the answer. No? OK, then, look outside of yourself. Look out of the window. Go on. There, out the back, hiding in the bushes. There is your answer. ENYA. She waits until you sleep, then sings her bloody awful doggerels like a tiny, mawkish, celtic buzzsaw, slicing through your slumber. Once your eyes open, she hides again, waiting for her next opportunity. DAMN YOU, ENYA, MAY MANKIND NEVER KNOW PEACE?!

Aquarius: Yet again, you awaken to a wholly-avoidable case of baboons in your vivarium. When will you learn? Oh, well. We'll talk about this later. Better go and get the story book. Baboons are getting sleepy.

Pisces: So, you constructed the palace made entirely out of drills, shaped like a giant drill, surrounded by orchards of genetically-adapted drill-trees, bathed in the light of stars which you had towed around the sky to form the outline of a giant drill. As you sit back on your drill-throne (bit uncomfortable, that one, not your finest hour) and sip from your drill-cocktail (like a screwdriver, but with red-bull in it, served - naturally - in a drill) you can't help but feel discontented. Only kidding, this is bloody brilliant. DRILLIANT! HAHA! DRILLS!

~

Your mind-cheeks are fat with pellets of eldritch knowledge! Chew on it slowly and keep yourself fed with powerful predictions for the week to come.

See you again soon, my furry little time-hamsters! Until then!

52

The week of December the 24th

Cometh the hour, cometh the badger! And such a bright-eyed little specimen you are, too! Now, sit your rump down and pin back those furry ear-holes, 'cos you're about to get a blast of future up you the likes of which I ought to charge for...

~

Aries: While wearing one of those coats with the fashionably-ironic elbow-patches sewn in, passing a college, you are mistaken for an actual geography teacher, grabbed by an irate-looking headmaster and instructed to get back in the room and start bloody well teaching people about Burma. Never again.

Taurus: Your nipples have names, you know. The right one is called 'Kennedy' and the left one is 'Zazu'. When you're sleeping, they sing to you, quietly, in French accents.

Gemini: Every where you go this week, you will be observed by a terrifying 6-foot-tall mallard called Flirty Bernard.

Cancer: Seek out meditative surroundings this week, places of healing. Your daily routine has become taxing and your energy reserves are low. Try finding somebody who enjoys cosplay and giving them a light, refreshing slap at a bus-stop. Fill a bowl with fruits, oils and wooden beads, then tip it over a goth. Lie back and completely shut-out the sound of an estate-agent being sodomized by highly-trained eagles. Relax.

Leo: You are soon to discover an entirely new flavour of soup, for which you are quickly arrested. That tinned broth industry's mighty cut-throat, buddy. Pay off the feds and move to the next state while the heat dies down.

Virgo: Love is in the air! You're suddenly head-over heels and throwing caution to the wind. After a few steamy dates, you soon find yourself back at your place, with the lights off, breathing heavily and being sensuously undressed by none other than Sandy Toksvig. She introduces you to an erotic wonderland of Lego and improvised comedy.

Libra: Your trousers are feeling increasingly aerodynamic of late. In practically any weather, the slightest gust of wind is enough to cause them to billow - a stiff breeze can see you lifting 3-4 inches off the ground, like a kind of improbable trouser kite. It may be recommendable to wear the specially-designed pant-weights for the next few days.

Scorpio: This week, you may only consume Kentucky Fried Chicken. Otherwise they will release the bears. The bears that find you delicious and have your address. OK? Only KFC. One week. Bears. Do it.

Sagittarius: Octopi are renowned for being skilled at camouflage, but few people realise the true depth of their talents. It is with these words in mind that the stars want you to hold tight for some really surprising news about your knickers.

Capricorn: Imagine your goal for the week. Concentrate on it. See yourself achieving this goal. Imagine the look on your face as you make this moment happen: the joy, the relief, the contentment. Imagine the look in your eyes as the clowns start filling the room. Hundreds and hundreds of clowns. Imagine the beads of sweat rolling down your face as the clowns surround you, pin you down, begin to paint you with glue and sequins. Imagine the darkness as they put you in the bag. Just imagine. Imagine. IMAGINE.

Aquarius: Oh, yes, Aquarius, you WILL play the bongos! Just like you always dreamed! Underwater, surrounded by penguins.

Pisces: The chase ends when you get cornered after completing your latest great work (making Big Ben into a MASSIVE drill bit and using it to drill a huge hole all the way through Penge). You drill down into the subway and flee to your underground lair, but still they hound you. Finally, you are forced to enter your escape pod and blast away to freedom... but ALAS! One of your stray drills (a really nice tungsten-carbide one) punctures the hull and your pod spins wildly out of control, crashing into the canopy of an unknown jungle, far from human voices. How will your story end? The stars wink and insist you will be riveted.

~

Good heavens, is that the time? I'm going to have to put these trousers back on and get out there. Police won't slather themselves in Marmite on their own, you know. Some of us have to work for a living.

Remember, the first rule of Horrorscopes: No Fight Club jokes.

SIGN PROFILES

ARIES

21st of March - 19th of April.

The Camper Van.

~

Most Compatible With: A brown, 1976 Austin Allegro.

Best Jobs: Academic, barber, politician.

Power Drink: Um Bongo (typically consumed in De Congo).

~

All Ariens are born with moustaches. It is partially because of this that they tend towards work in administrative roles, though they are also skilled pornographers and make deeply corrupt ombudsmen. Until the mid 1600s, it was thought that those born of this sign had a natural affinity to tweed. Closer scrutiny eventually revealed this to be their skin, which, owing to a common ancestor (thought to have been a Geography teacher) has a brownish hue, regardless of exposure to the sun.

Over 70% of Ariens are Canadian, due to complex climate-related issues and the obscure breeding rituals prevalent in Canada. In Bolivia, through the 1980s, there was only one child born under the sign of Aries. Known as 'Lucky Bob', he is most commonly known as the inventor of under-water tromboning, for which he holds several world records.

Ariens tend toward being tall and middle-class, sexually depraved and keen philatelists. It is impossible to convince an Aries to enter a church (not because of any antipathy regarding religion, but due to a strong perceived link between Churches and the highly political musical work of Public Enemy).

Most Ariens have a small switch on their back which can be used to put them in 'power saving mode', during the operation of which, they will be unable to walk faster than a casual saunter, but can go for over three weeks on a single bag of Wotsits.

~

Likes: The classic Aries child will naturally gravitate toward collections of magazines about wood, carefully sorted piles of bark, photographs of Polish people, apes and Mardi Gras. Boiled sweets are often popular, and for holiday destinations, the Aries will almost always choose Dunstable.

Hates: Owing to a fundamental inability to tolerate hip-hop, most born of this sign display an intense allergic reaction when brought into contact with Flavour Flav and funk of any sort is known to be met with confused indifference. Ariens also exhibit dismay when exposed to football as they fear spheres which bring them near to tears.

Love: To woo an Aries, it is written that one must first coax them out of their nest by playing freestyle jazz and talking earnestly about the economy, Europe and caravans. Relationships with Ariens are long and tedious, leading more commonly to suicide than divorce.

Money: Frugal and ambivalent, the Aries is prone toward saving and is extremely cautious in business. The only fiduciary blind-spot for people of this sign appears to be for polished oak dildos, which they are drawn to (often from extreme distances) and will immediately purchase and cherish.

Luck: Generally poor. If you spy an Aries placing a bet, a wise man would immediately place the opposite bet, then run away and hide under a large concrete hedgehog.

Famous Ariens: Belinda Carlisle. Sting. Gordon Brown. Chewbacca the Wookie. Dale Winton. Kent.

TAURUS

20th of April - 20th of May.

The Pregnant Kestrel.

~

Most Compatible With: MEAT.

Best Jobs: Chef, boxer, astrophysicist.

Power Drink: Cheetah's wee-wee.

~

Taurus, according to Greek legend, was an ancient half-man, half-anchovy who scaled Mount Olympus to steal chips from the Gods and bring them back to East London. For this reason, all Taureans smell faintly of cooking oil and are almost exclusively Cockneys.

Taureans, due to their unusual diet, are often blessed with the power of vision, allowing their brains to interpret the interaction of light beams with sensitive cells formed on the inside of what scientists are now calling their 'eyes', recognising simple letters and flying into rages when they see a waggling red rag.

Unfortunately, the opposite of the adage about blind peoples' hearing improving to compensate for their loss is true and those born under Taurus are universally deaf as a post, due to their freakishly-developed eyes.

When cornered, it is typical to find that a Taurean will adopt a slightly racist Greek accent and attempt to interest the predator in a kebab, using the word 'innit' almost four thousand times per minute, innit.

The sign of Taurus is widely regarded as one of the most homoerotic, with those falling under this sign regularly stripping to their waist in the street, oiling themselves and proceeding to solve even the most minor of discussions with scarily over-enthusiastic bouts of wrestling.

Taureans often affect a natural, forest-inspired look, styling their hair into fronds and leaves, singing songs about foliage and idolising the work and hair-do of Adolf Hitler. It is rarely a wise idea to question the link between these topics as a smack in the mouth is typically not far away when dealing with these cantankerous oafs.

~

Likes: Tat. Pound shops. Television programs about people who buy shite and sell it off at a minuscule profit. Taureans are renowned for their love of thrift and working class people with orange skin. Documentaries about homosexual racists. Tartan turbans. Voles. Donuts.

Hates: The Fiesta 1.1 Popular Plus, Brillo pads, trifle, gurning. Being the last person to get picked at an orgy. The number 41. Cornflakes.

Love: Taureans adore marzipan to a near-sexual degree. Each week, they can be found stalking around the deserted desert aisles of major local supermarkets, attempting to capture and slay wild marzipan deer that they believe to exist. During these times, they are easily corralled and impregnated.

Money: Absolutely made of it! Every Taurus sits upon a small pot of gold, living (as they do) at the ends of rainbows. Repeatedly punching a Taurus in the face while screaming "Give me the gold, you tiny green bastard" is thought to cause the Taurus to emit golden vomit, whereas stroking their reproductive organs vigorously is said to cause them to ejaculate pound coins.

Luck: Variable. It is said that associating closely with a Taurus is much like riding a rollercoaster, run by a half-blind pervert. Take off your trousers, hold tight and whatever you do, don't look down.

Famous Taureans: Tom Cruise. Ant and Dec. Father Christmas. Denzel Washington. Cashew nuts. Spain.

GEMINI

21st of May - 20th of June.

The Flapping Wound.

~

Most Compatible With: The Commodore 64 parallel printer port.

Best Jobs: Gemini are most suited to working in unisex toilets, attempting to bully people into giving them money for unwanted fragrances and even more unwanted verbal abuse. When not performing the function of 'bog troll' for the local discotheque, Gemini are often found sauntering back and forth in front of televisions in electronics shops, declaring loudly how "this one has really good anamorphic, yep, yep, really good ratio" to nobody in particular.

Power Drink: Bovril.

~

Those born under the sign of Gemini are often

on the flimsy side - some lighter than air itself. It is a well-known phenomenon that left untethered, approximately 40% of Geminis float off into the stratosphere. Fortunately, due to an arrangement with Father Christmas, any stray Gemini children that escape their moorings are rounded up and herded back to their owners by flying Space Wasps. The wasps do not enjoy the work and often sting the children, which is one of the many reasons Geminis have such an appalling sense of humour. A few brushes with the space wasps usually leaves them pretty much sick of the world. Plus, Santa charges a rather hefty admin-fee for these duties, which the parents of Geminis often feel are largely the fault of the child themselves and it is customary to present them with a large bill on their 18th birthday.

Despite these negatives, nearly all Geminis survive childhood as they are, of course, bulletproof. Though light as a feather, their exteriors are constructed from a space-age meta-material known only as Kynoch's Odour, thought to be distilled from the bitter tears of a middle-school maths teacher, dripped delicately onto a mould and left to harden. This is also why all Gemini children look exactly the same. It is only later in life that the mould begins to crack, once the individual has reached the age of adulthood. Unsheathed, the young adult will begin to differentiate him/herself from their brethren, often by means of an improvised sporran or hair net, painted in the colour of the Gemini: ultra-violet.

This habit makes it preposterously easy to find any Gemini players in a game of hide and seek, assuming you have an ultra-violet lamp. Shining it around the area immediately causes all nearby Geminis to fluoresce. This is typically not necessary, though, as it is almost impossible to teach Gemini children how to play and enjoy games, as they shun all forms of entertainment besides their favourite activity of "Guess how many oats are in the bag". They always play and always win this game, though it is suggested that this may be because nobody else wishes to play.

~

Likes: The sound of rain falling on an orphan. Italian porn stars who become politicians. Italian politicians who become porn stars. Scooby Doo (but not Scrappy Doo - Geminis are not monsters). Tizwaz. Elves. Cheese-flavoured maize snacks. Teasing obese children with ice-cream. Having sex while wearing a khaghoul.

Hates: Thumb wars with tramps. When you try to get into a tin can with one of those old can-openers and the top ends up tattered and rent like a bin that's been bummed by a horny Transformer. Acoustic dubstep. Reality television. Calculus.

Love: It is not possible to truly love a Gemini, owing to their extraordinary facial deformities, staggering misanthropy and pungent odour, many have engaged them in purely sexual relationships and escaped with their lives, if not their dignity. The best way to attract the attention of a Gemini is to stare fixedly at their genitals while emitting a low grunting sound. Once aroused, the Gemini must be taken roughly and uncompromisingly up the Richard before their sedatives wear off and they become dangerous.

Money: It's either feast or fast with these people. Either rolling in filthy lucre or wanking off tramps for copper coins. A windfall is quickly frittered away, but weirdly, another bout of good luck, a win on the nags or an unsuspecting student with a glass jaw is never far away. Thus the coffers are refilled.

Luck: Geminis have literally no luck. Not bad luck, but a net average of zero positive or negative change due to luck. If they were to play a one-armed bandit 100 times, the Gemini would leave with exactly the same amount of money with which they began. For this reason, they are not allowed in casinos as they are considered a bloody irritating waste of time.

Famous Geminis: Sir Patrick Stewart. Bear Grylls. The entire cast of Monty Python. Pat Sharp. Bognor Regis. Lime Regis. Walnuts.

Cancer

22nd of June - 22nd of July.

The asymmetrical hairdo.

~

Most Compatible With: The bronze era.

Best Jobs: Cancerians are often employed as replacement members of Boyzone. They are fresh-faced and boyish (even/particularly the women), have a 'cheeky' (irritating) attitude and manner of speech and are blessedly free of any sort of cranial complication that might make them go off-piste. A Cancerian employee will do what you tell them, even if what you tell them to do is to nibble off their own left leg, if only because no intervening thought is likely to occur to them over the course of the day.

Power Drink: Selotape, melted down into a plastic paste, then stirred up with some bubbling hot goose fat into a drink they refer to as "Pling".

~

All Cancerians are born with their own unique theme tune and are able to whistle it immediately from birth onwards. In some situations, it can become incredibly difficult to prevent them from whistling or humming it loudly as a sort of verbal tick, for instance, if they feel anxious. Or aroused.

As children, Cancerians will be popular with everybody. This is less to do with their personalities, which are often shrill and demeaning and more to do with the fact that they slowly emit highland toffee from the pores of their skin. This can lead to a build-up of acquaintances who merely follow the child with a bucket (or in the case of more enterprising children, a fork-lift truck) to catch the toffee, so that it may later be sold on at profit. The McCowan's company has successfully harnessed the power of young Cancerian children for hundreds of years, with each of their factories comprising a few such youngsters dangled upside down and repeatedly scolded by a staff-member wearing the appropriate safety equipment (plus ear-baffles to defend against the high-pitched hooting noises and deeply personal insults the child gives off under these circumstances).

Inevitably, young Cancerian children learn to escape their bonds or bribe their captors with free toffee and almost all survive to maturity, at which point the toffee-production tapers off. It is at this juncture that the biology of the adult Cancerian begins to synthesise Sherbert Dip Dab and the cycle proceeds similarly, but with larger harnesses required and usually in factories around Sheffield and the Midlands. Initially, the migration of Cancerians over their lifetime was thought to be an innate instinct, an attempt to find a mate and raise them in a nest which they might weave from scraps of paper picked from litter bins or bright wool and thread stolen from a haberdashery. In recent years, however, this hypothesis was disproven as GPS tagging enabled more precise tracking of the individuals and showed that in successive escapes from factory life, there was merely an urge to head to the South because "it's less grim there" and, as one youngster put it, "they don't keep locking us up in bloody toffee factories".

Of course, when the adult reaches the southernmost point of the landmass, they are ritually thrown into the sea as has been legally required for the last century, following the rule of King Bernard the Arbitrary.

~

Likes: Pasta, mischief, the Welsh. If you intend to lure a Cancerian into a trap (or relationship) (or both) then a common tactic is to leave a piping hot spaghetti bolognaise out next to a television showing repeats of 90s tv 'humour' show 'Candid Camera', beneath a large iron cage. Iron is used in the entrapment procedure owing to the Cancerian's fundamental affinity toward other common metals and ability to sing to the bars of (say) a silver cage and convince them to bend.

Hates: Knitting (waste of good nesting-wool), herbivores, Canon office equipment (particularly printers/scanners, but anything bearing the mark will raise suspicion and contempt if not outright blood-lust).

Love: Cancerians are complex lovers owing to a naturally oscillating sexuality. On alternate weeks, they move from being straight, to bisexual, to powerfully gay, then back to bisexual again, on a near-monthly rotation. This does mean that three individuals of the same sign, if appropriately synchronised, can form a polygamous relationship that will wether the test of time, with two partners always fully up for each other and one simply relegated to watching sport for the contentious weeks.

Money: Disastrous. Cancerians feel immediately impelled to invest all of their worldly currency into Bitcoin at atrocious conversion rates, which they then attempt to use to buy chicken. They simply cannot be convinced that chicken is legal and may be purchased over the counter in most countries of the world. They're having none of it. Steer clear.

Luck: The luck of this star sign is entirely dependent on the colour of lighting in the individual's environment. If surrounded by cool hues - blues and purples, their luck is generally tremendous and they will happily buy everybody chips on the proceeds. If, however, they find themselves under the glare of red lamps (such as those employed to display the wares of a local prostitute) then all is doomed and the result of practically any betting scenario is death.

Famous Cancerians: Cheryl Cole. Prince. Frank Skinner. Jemima Puddleduck. France. Ovaltine.

LEO

21st of March - 19th of April.

The unicorn's balls.

~

Most Compatible With: Sticklebricks.

Best Jobs: There's no way around it, Leos are best at fighting. It's their calling. The only thing they don't often realise is that they're best at fighting whelks, not people. Put a Leo in a ring against two, three, even four whelks and they will take those slimy little bastards to pieces. Five and upwards and things may start to get hairy, but four and below, your Leo's coming out on top. Most Leos tend to find themselves employed by clubs in seaside villages, to keep the Friday night trouble under control.

Power Drink: Sea Brine with a splash of sailor's tears. They can tell which is which.

~

Your typical common or garden Leo is a cocky individual. They're street smart, they've got a killer perm and that fresh-off-the-sunbed tan and they know they're going to break hearts. This is unfortunate as the average Leo is also a little under four foot tall and all have cleft palates and double-jointed knees that regularly over-extend, resulting in a perverse, stooping, bobbing gait that is regularly mistaken for a weirdly inappropriate John Cleese impression.

What they lack in stature, they do make up for in potatoes. Leos know where to find themselves a potato at any time of the AM. Afternoons and evenings, not so great. Mornings? Check. Any time after midnight, in fact, right up until noon. The origin of this spectacular and desirable ability stems from their oddly-developed frontal cortex. Research on Leos has shown that in every tested subject to date, the Leo brain has an additional nodule toward the front of the mind-box, shaped like a walnut. It was only recently discovered on account of the way that walnuts look rather a lot like brains, a form of natural camouflage.

Leos are resilient, trustworthy and always lean over toward the left on a Thursday. If you want an honest opinion about a new hat you've purchased, ask a Leo. It's not that they are free of guile or social misdirection but long, long ago, when the Earth was still young, Terry, King of the Leos swore a blood oath with the mighty Goddess Hera that he would never again be dishonest in his opinion about headwear after a catastrophic war resulted from a little white lie he had employed to weasel out of mentioning that

Her fascinator looked ridiculous.

If you meet a Leo and learn their True Name (it's sewn inside their socks, for instance) then you may proclaim it to them in the format "Ha ha, you filthy bastard - your true name is [insert name here] and I want what's coming to me!" - and they will be legally obliged to bestow upon you a boon. This is most commonly used to get Leos to get a round in, something they have a tendency to avoid, on account of being tight.

~

Likes: Belgium, snakes, voodoo and films beginning with the letter 'Q'. It is hard to please a Leo, but you generally won't need to as they stockpile all of the things that make them happy and keep them in a box underneath their bed which they guard viciously. Not really from anybody, because nobody wants their stuff.

Hates: Belgians, rakes, U2 and kilns baking red-setter poo. If you really do want to raise the dander of a Leo, you could always go and nick their box from under the bed, but genuinely, it's not worth the belly-aching. They just won't leave it alone, all "OMG you took the only things in the world that make me happy, now I have no purpose left in life" - waa waa waa.

Love: Ah, the noble Leo as a partner! Few survive this wild ride. Few dare try. But if you've got a thing for midgets with enormous attitude problems, you might find the diminutive grumbling wretch for you! To steal their heart, simply mention to them that you have a large lead chest under your floorboards that you are prepared to allow them to rent and tattoo the words "straddle me, you love god" onto your face. They will find you irresistible.

Money: Leo can always be relied upon to have a healthy bank balance and to pay their bills on time. They won't pay anybody else's bills, they'll argue every last cent of an attempt to split a bill and hunt you down remorselessly and stare at you meaningfully for hours with the cold, ruthless eyes of a killer if you are so stupid as to borrow money from them, but in terms of looking after their own shit, Leos be on point.

Luck: Actually quite lucky. Perhaps the gods look down upon the tiny, misshapen heads of Leos and think "you know what? They've had a tough day. Give them a break." Maybe it's simply that fate wants little to do with them. Either way, Leos tend to be some lucky sons of bitches.

Famous Leos: Both Butch Cassidy and the Sundance Kid. Milli Vanilli. Oprah Winfrey. Gordon the Gopher. Lembit Opik. The Terrahawks. Bletchley Park.

VIRGO

23rd of August - 22nd of September.

The pregnant lesbian.

~

Most Compatible With: The Black and Decker Workmate™ (original model, not the new plastic one, you joker).

Best Jobs: Butler, lion-tamer, cake decorator, priest. They like to do things with their hands, and that's precisely why you should give them a job that keeps those hands busy. If you don't, they'll find something to do with them and you're guaranteed to wish they hadn't. Capable of complex and abstract work if filled with sufficient stimulants. Without, as torpid as a bag of plums.

Power Drink: A steaming pint of mead, poured from a brazed barrel.

~

It is not easy to describe the personality of the average Virgo, as no ready comparison exists. They are the best of us and yet the worst of us. They have genitals so large and powerful they can destroy cities with a momentary mucky thought, yet they are often so hideous and malodorous that even the beasts of the field rebuke their attempts at love-play. They are loyal and loving as a wasp. A big, angry, horny wasp that just wants to show you a good time look why are you crying OK fine I'll leave. That sorta deal.

Virgos are also prone to bursts of emotion (anger), frustration (anger) and poorly-expressed anxiety (anger) if they are not gratified sexually on an hourly basis. Teams of trained fluffers are often hired to traipse around behind Virgoans, ready at a moment's notice to help them crack one off before Shit Gets Real. Of course, highly-skilled fluffer-troupes don't come cheap, but fortunately, Virgoans are rarely out of employment for long. Using a combination of deceit, card-tricks, outright lies and a pair of old shoes they found nailed to a bit of wood, they are able to pass almost any interview and inveigle themselves into positions of power from whence they are powerfully difficult to unseat.

If all this sounds like bad news, the typical Virgo does at least have one single redeeming quality, which is that they make some of the most bewilderingly delicious trifles known to man. Their methods are highly secretive and many reporters have been 'lost' in the field, attempting to track down the recipe or even rough outline of ingredients - sometimes their bodies are recovered, set into a mouth-watering fruit jelly as a warning - but whatever it is they do, they're not telling. Most people think they just get ten large cheap ones from a shop and put them in a bin for a while. Never suggest this to their face.

~

Likes: Handcuffs. Jelly. Multiples of five. In most things, the Virgoan outlook is one of simplicity. They simply want the most complex, ridiculous, overly difficult set of things, they want them now and if they can't have them then they will have a big cry until somebody does something about it.

Hates: The dark, being forced into packing containers and repeatedly called 'Susan', Elves. Anything that is not about them is the rule of thumb for discerning what might or might not cause a Virgo to start literally shitting blood at the drop of a hat. If it's an Elf's hat at night, consider that hat to be bloodily shat in.

Love: It can be easy to love a Virgo. All you really have to do is agree with them. They're so utterly besotted with themselves - the sound of their own voice, their eyes meeting their own eyes across a crowded bar, etc - that if you smile and nod at the right places, they'll think you have wonderful taste and probably end up inviting you back for a threesome (you, them and their terrifyingly warped ego).

Money: A Virgo and their money are... well, unlikely. The sort of person who spends next month's paycheque on tarts and gin before this month's bills have got a look in. If you have the opportunity to go into business with a Virgoan partner, a wise technique to prevent yourself from falling into problems with money is to quickly and efficiently shoot them through the head. You must sever the brainstem, or they are still able to order things online.

Luck: Lucky as they come 99% of the time, then spastically, terrifyingly, world-shatteringly unlucky about once a year, but pretty much at the moment where it will be the most inconvenient. The trouble is knowing when this actually is. It might be best to simply follow from a short distance and see if they step on a land-mine or somehow effortlessly style it all out again.

Famous Virgoans: Bob Carolgees. Mister Smithers. Aneka Rice. Terminators 1 and 3. Derby County Council. Chief Chirpa of the Ewoks. The decimal fraction 5.5622389.

LIBRA

23rd of September - 23rd of October.

The Phallic Candelabra.

~

Most Compatible With: Robots / the clergy / the robot clergy.

Best Jobs: Bell-ringer, slurry watchman, Casio VL-Tone tuning mechanic.

Power Drink: Lucozade Sport mixed with the blood of virgins.

~

It is a common suggestion of those who attribute the sign of the scales to Librans, that they represent balance, assessment and fairness. Of course, this is a huge mistake and nothing could be further from the truth. If their sign really means anything about their personalities, it would indicate in some way that those born betwixt September and October like vigorously plunging themselves in and out of sticky situations. This is, at least, to some degree true.

Librans are ambidextrous, androgynous and absolutely ambivalent. It's possible, if futile, to arouse their enthusiasms (for they do exist) but most people will find the Librans they know tucked away behind a copy of the Dandy, humming tunelessly while absent-mindedly feeding themselves from a tub of honeycomb (often placed there by a butler or well-meaning friend). They will, if allowed, follow their nesting instinct and begin to create a sort of make-do hutch or bivouac inside a nearby shed (or Wendy house). During the winter, they will retreat to this cozy den and emit a low cooing sound if disturbed. Finally, in the spring, the fully hibernated Libran will emerge, dressed in Emo fashion and only responding to the name "Kurt". A few weeks later, they will be entirely back to normal and later in the year, the whole process repeats again ad infinitum.

In outward appearance, most Librans resemble a 14 to 17 year old girl, but with a soft, downy fur on their arms and back. They respond poorly to bright sunlight but are not allergic. If asked they will merely claim to find the sun passé and "completely failing to innovate in recent years". It is thought that in the pre-history of man, some sort of super-dense proto-Libran may have bred with another compatible species to form what we now know as Goths, but this has yet to be proven. Librans are, of course, deeply suspicious of owls and competitive sport.

Likes: The sound of sea birds. Fingering valves. Letting it all hang out. The typical Libran can be won over into a friend for life by plying them with midget gems and the music of the Aphex Twin (early stuff, any way - Selected Ambient Works II is a good bet).

Hates: Corrugated iron, Parma Violets, the texture of lumpy custard. Connections (spiritual or aesthetic) with anything that was really popular in the '70s. Gurgling. Anything that reminds them too strongly of the physical life they crave to leave behind. Any form of taxation or official correspondence.

Love: Courting a Libran can be rewarding if you are prepared to tolerate their habits. Apart from their tolerant nature (they will ignore most things if left in their daydream world of butterflies and colourful stimulus), it is possible to shave them regularly and retire upon the proceeds of their wool. As many do.

Money: Librans have no concept of money, but it can be used to distract them by taping shiny coins to the end of a thread and dangling it before their hypnotised faces. The same, however, can be achieved with tin foil / bottle caps / Twix wrappers / moist wood.

Luck: Not really of a dependable quality of luck, Librans are, however, popular as mascots. Sometimes, when attached to the prow of a ship, or tied to the roof rack of a Ford Cortina, they have been known to smile benignly upon harvests, races or amateur attempts at genetic experimentation, leading to an overwhelming feeling of contentment and good-natured bon-homie. This is, though, illusory and inevitably ends in death.

Famous Librans: Captain Bravestarr. The Nolan Sisters. Chuck D (though not Flava Flav, despite popular rumour). Sore nipples at bedtime. Tamworth.

SCORPIO

October 24th - November 21st.

The Fragrant Unicycle.

~

Most Compatible With: That special coloured grit you put in fish bowls.

Best Jobs: Believe themselves to be the walking incarnation of Leonardo Da Vinci, but often best employed as a floppy lump for holding down a tarpaulin in a stiff breeze, or perhaps giving a dog something harmless to bite.

Power Drink: Pencil shavings and froth.

~

Prone to the unbuttoned cuff (and shirt, and pants), these Johnny-come-latelys of the Zodiac waft into social situations, like the odour of a rich gentleman's fart (meaty and expensive). Rarely invited, but regularly present, they swan about the gaff acting as though they not only own the place but intend to sell it for below the asking price just to show how little anything really means to them.

This effete nihilism is, however, a sham - and an easily exposed one at that. If you were to take the precious things of a Scorpio (their bangra CDs, or finely patterned disco-trousers bought from a long-dead street Guru on Brick Lane) and dangle them over an open flame, you would soon hear their weeping lament, desperate cries and promises of rich rewards to take save their coveted gewgaws. They loves their shinies and they're bloody rubbish at hiding it.

The throw-away aesthetic doesn't end with material goods, though, as the souls of the Scorpio are profoundly lacking, too. They barely read, enjoy the music of Oasis and if held at knife-point and presented with the choice between reciting as many digits of Pi as they could muster or facing instant termination, their only cogent answer would be "I like cake. It is brown." They are, of course, imbeciles, with floppy legs and a handshake like a muskrat bleeding out.

Despite these qualities, Scorpios make surprisingly good company. They don't really care what you say about them (if indeed they comprehend, which they don't), they fill gaps in the conversation (by talking about some amazing new art piece they're going to make in a hedge in Milton Keynes) and they are the perfect confidant as they never actually listen to anything anybody says to them. Should you tire of the company of a Scorpio, simply position them in front of a full-length mirror, where they will caw, wink and preen appreciatively until covered with a dark cloth.

~

Likes: Penzance. The music of Funkdoobiest. Expensive packs of felt-tipped pens (the ones that come with more than one black pen). Running around the woods at the weekend, shouting "I AM LEGOLAS AND I WILL BE YOUR ELVEN HERO, MILADY" ... Shouting the same thing at the moment of climax. Or in the chemist.

Hates: Pendulums. Actual scorpions (which, if spotted, they will dance around, taunting and calling 'six-legged twats', often fatally). Open source software initiatives. Neckerchiefs. The sound of a harp being vigorously strummed by a love-struck baboon. China Crisis. The feel of corduroy against their cheeks.

Love: Scorpios make fantastic, passionate, attentive and overwhelmingly skilled lovers. In reality, I only wrote the previous sentence because those words have never before and will never again be found in the English language, in that order, in any context. Sex with a Scorpio is like repeatedly combing your genitals with an old rake. Their idea of romance is the entire Friends boxed DVD set and a packet of walnuts (which they often forget).

Money: Despite earning little, Scorpios are frugal and, like a financial dolphin, able to go for long periods of time without shopping. It's thought they might have some sort of rudimentary gills that allow them to extract small change from the air as they walk around. Again, in much the way dolphins do.

Luck: Ridiculously lucky, on account of having a fundamental idiocy about the nature of statistics. These people truly do not understand that you can't keep playing probability and winning over and over again, and as a result somehow get away with it. To the utter disgust and contempt of their contemporaries (which they utterly fail to notice).

Famous Scorpios: Ini Kamoze, Bob Monkhouse, all members of the original lineup of Ned's Atomic Dustbin, the planet Neptune, parmesan, Woking.

SAGITTARIUS

November 22nd - December 21st

The rotating valve.

~

Most Compatible With: Spoons which have been assigned unusual romantic significance.

Best Jobs: Workin' in a coal mine. Goin' down down down. Workin' in a coal mine. Whoop! about to slip down. Sorry, we meant 'estate agent'.

Power Drink: Babycham with just a dash of Brut.

~

In the olden times, when man had barely left the caves and still bore his vestigial tail, Sagittarians roamed the earth freely and were often believed to be an entirely different species. Part lizard, part mammal, part administrative clerk, the Dark Ones slunk around early hominid encampments, stealing food from tables, sometimes daring to try to drag away a human child for their sustenance. They would be fought off or simply urinated on copiously, but were tenacious and slowly became tolerated, if not accepted, by early man and his kin.

In some parts of the country, enterprising youngsters have successfully saddled wild Sagittarians and claim to have achieved speeds upwards of 3mph in open country, though this practice is considered dangerous and most police-forces will attempt to shutdown gatherings of "Sagi-Handlers" or "Valve-Teasers" before events get out of hand. In even more clandestine meetings, those familiar with a Sagittarian have been known to bring them to closed-group meetings in darkened buildings on the outskirts of civilisation, coax them into taking position in special made restraining-harnesses and at great risk to personal safety, extracted their milk.

This is, of course, pointless, as their milk is nothing to write home about: slightly bitter and prone to curdling. Much like the people.

When not being yoked, trapped, manipulated or slandered like scaly pre-human cattle from times ill-remembered, Sagittarians are prone to agency-work of all kinds. Whether it be the resale of horrible houses at extortionate profit or humans into near-indentured wage-slavery, this grim lot are ideally suited to the sort of work that requires an intrinsic distrust of people coupled with the understanding that they must nestle close to humanity's warming light or otherwise perish. In worst cases, some have been known to work in gymnasiums as personal instructors.

~

Likes: Carrot cake, the Cocteau Twins, Dr Robotnik. The things of the past hold sway in the affections of the Sagittarius - the topics and items long forgotten except in ancient, blind, racial dreams of when we once all swam together in the darkness. That, and they are partial to Toblerone.

Hates: Candy-floss, unpaid invoices, all of the actors in the popular Doctor Who spin-off series Torchwood. The laughter of children makes them particularly crotchety and not a little bit peckish. For some reason, they are also fiercely protective of bin-men and have been known to rear up and flail wildly with their pronounced talons when seeing them harassed.

Love: It was one thought that only another part-lizard hybrid wretch could love a creature such as a Sagittarian, but as in all domains, life and a very horny, very drunk farmer will find a way. Evidence increasingly points toward successful attempts to breed with the beasts, but it is beyond the scope of this (or any) journal to detail the procedure. There are some things a man must not see.

Money: Weirdly, the Sagittarius has a particularly fine grasp on money and is often seen checking the balance on their ISA so that they can squirrel away a few more pounds at a low tax level. This seems at odds with their backwards demeanour and nobody knows what they plan to spend their (clearly) ill-gotten gains on, yet still they hoard.

Luck: There is certainly nothing considered lucky about being born under this sign, or the "Zodiac's arse", but at the same time, despite all the odds, like the lingering smell at the bottom of the bin that remains despite cleansing it with bleach, acid, and eventually replacing the bin, still they persist. Somebody somewhere must be smiling on them. If only we knew whom.

Famous Sagittarians: Ghandi, Stalin, Beatrix Potter, Fortnum and Mason, Stelios Haji-Ioannou, Barnstaple Town Council and Rotary Club, Whitby.

CAPRICORN

December 22nd - January 19th

The astronaut and gherkin.

~

Most Compatible With: Leopards / bank managers / leopard managers.

Best Jobs: Dreamer, day-dreamer, salesman, arch-bishop. Hypnotising the masses and selling them their own buttocks if necessary.

Power Drink: Somebody else's coffee.

~

Ah, the noble, flighty Capricorn! Like a whirlwind of hair and expectations, they swoop into the lives of their friends, family and colleagues, deliver a million tiny bomblets of inspiration and unreasonable demands, then ascend once more to the heavens to live among their true brethren, the clouds, while everybody stands about asking what just happened.

Those born of this sign are constituted in equal parts of candy floss, genius, mania, espresso and expensive shoes. Like a human chameleon, they are able to talk to prince and pauper, both, and will leave both wondering where they can obtain such powerful drugs on the black market. While known (and loved) for their firm, powerful buttocks (reminiscent of those of a big cat, perhaps a panther), they are also enjoyed for their small yet perky nipples and abundant chest hair (particularly among the ladies).

Often introduced as a mover and/or shaker in a given scene / party / business meeting / love-making session, the real calling of the Capricorn is to act as a larger-than-life, walking-talking distraction from whatever it was that was getting everybody down. Like a sort of short-term ecstasy pill, for the length of a conversation, these unique and flavoursome individuals can make even the most down-to-earth grumbler soar into whimsy. Of course, there is always a price and the conversational comedown has been known to leave those unable to deal with it frazzled and limp, forcing themselves to watch endless episodes of children's cartoons and gorge on pop-tarts in a vague attempt to regain some much-needed seratonin.

Capricorns like to live high up. If a penthouse flat can't be afforded, they will make their nest in the tallest tree in the forest. Or stand on a box, complaining loudly but with scintillating form, until somebody offers them somewhere nicer to be in the hope of shutting them up. This has the joint advantage of them being able to adopt their favourite position of gazing down upon the world, while also furnishing the world with a fantastic view of their legendary buttocks.

It is said that if you shave a Capricorn from head to foot they will be really irritated.

~

Likes: Shiny things. These must be curated, obtained, purloined or otherwise acquired and woven into a fine and sparkling nest in which the Capricorn's young may nest and grow fat, surrounded by glistening, confusing baubles when just a normal house would have been entirely acceptable.

Hates: Unexpectedly cold lattes, Tax returns, being told "that really isn't possible, we just don't have enough fudge to make the entire statue", overly restrictive trousers, cold winters (cold summers even more).

Love: Don't even go there. Oh, they'll love you alright. They'll love you so hard, so passionately, so deeply that you'll think you've never been loved before, like you never even knew what the word meant, like you never want it to stop and like you'll never be able to love again if it does. And then there's the sound of squealing tyres and all that's left is a hand full of luke-warm sex-custard, a wad of fifty pound notes and the words 'Tweet me'. Bastard.

Money: Don't even go there. See above. Actually, money does not truly exist for the Capricorn, other than as a form of conversation that ideally other people have while they go base-jumping off a scale model of the Eiffel tower, made out of diamonds that they got installed in their bathroom in case things got too mundane on a Thursday.

Luck: Bewilderingly lucky, with occasional exceptions regarding parking tickets or the occasional vietnamese dominatrix whose sub par grasp of Klingon almost spoils the passion. Anything that goes wrong for a Capricorn can be fixed, though. They have people for that sort of thing...

Famous Capricorns: Leonardo DiCaprio, captain Pugwash, Donald Trump, Arthur Daley. The new Pentium 12 Velocibastard. Knightsbridge.

AQUARIUS

January 20th - February 18th

The majestic stilton.

~

Most Compatible With: Bob Hoskins / Bob Carolgees.

Best Jobs: Selling leather to a man. Barrowing things. Watching the till at an all-night trouser emporium in the middle of Soho.

Power Drink: Aloe Vera (with bits).

~

Diminutive and swarthy of appearance, the Aquarean is practically born into a hoodie. One of nature's instinctive lurkers, it's a common thing to not be entirely sure what an Aquarean's face looks like despite knowing them quite well, as it is so regularly occluded by a crafty cigarette, pasty of dubious provenance, mobile phone (of extremely dubious provenance) or gambling periodical. If you want a pair of trainers, top of the line, twenty quid, no questions asked, tap them up. They've got a pair with them as it happens, or they know a lad who has. Or they can get some if you want. What do you mean, like the ones that chap's wearing? Give us a minute.

If you don't know what they do for a living (or better yet - in the daytime) then it's really best not to ask. It's probably legal, but probably not very. There's probably meat of some sort involved. Imported meat. I've already said too much. You didn't hear about this from me. Let's change the subject.

Should a member of your family be born under this sign, then you will know that they are loyal, if uncomplicated, and as children, liked to play in the hedge (where they said they were talking to their friends - which you assume were hopefully hedgehogs or something). Recent interactions with the animal kingdom are more likely to be owning some sort of demented half-breed dog (the latter being assumed, they will look like the product of a weasel fucking a skateboard) which you suspect smokes rollups, answers to absolutely any name whatsoever and eats kids. Other interactions are now mostly limited to pointing at other animals (dead or alive) for Oy-ScruffyBollocks to chase down, maul and consume noisily.

Interpersonal relationships are mostly warm, if repetitive. Conversation tends to sound as though they only have ten things they can ask you about, which they will do, day or night, whether you spoke to them two years or five seconds ago, relentlessly. At least five of them are "You alright then, mate?" The generally amiable demeanour can change in a heartbeat if a fellow were to accidentally pick up the wrong pint, or hand over 20p too little in change, or suggest that the pasty they just consumed might not have met with the rigorous health and safety standards enjoyed by most popular eateries. In such a situation, it's wise to keep one eye on the door. And the other on the dog.

These moments, though, are fleeting, as most people seek rapidly to make recompense once dealt with, the matter is immediately forgotten and glossed over by a cheery "You alright then, mate?"

∾

Likes: Snouts, darkness, cubby holes, Adidas, haggling and (disconcertingly) the Times cryptic crossword ("Keeps the brain going, innit? You alright then, bruv?") Also keen on the let's-assume-it's-a-dog, which seems to be pretty much attached to the end of their jeans. Football (not a specific team, "I just enjoy it for the spectacle, isn't it? You alright then, boss?")

Hates: Italian women (for a number of nuanced and complicated reasons that do not bear repeating in polite company), lemons ("They is well zesty. You good though, mate?"), not charging for credit card transactions, honeysuckle ("It puts me in mind of a cool evening in the meadows, which is mental 'cos I ain't ever been to no meadows, and anyway, that imagery is well melancholy, right? You well though, bruv?"), more than two children in the shop.

Love: The first thing to consider when planning to engage in relations with an Aquarius is "What will I do to distract the dog?" - the second logically follows, then, as "And if we get together, where will it live?" The answer to either question has put off many a budding Aquarean romance. If, however, you're a dog person and you know where you can get hold of some mint tracksuit bottoms, right, slip the pooch a packet of sausages and go find out what they're keeping under that zipper.

Money: Stable and reliable cash-flow is a focal point of each and every day with the Aquarean. You will be moderately well-furnished for the remainder of your years if you manage to successfully negotiate a relationship with such a being. On the other hand, if you try to haggle with them, you might well find yourself paying twice the original asking price, plus agreeing to buy a carton of Camels you weren't interested in (if indeed you even smoke).

Luck: Aquareans seem to have the gift of the gab (albeit in their limited fashion) and a strange likeability, combined with a terrifying hell-dog and lethal bargaining skills. They don't necessarily shoot for the stars, but life tends to look after them to a greater or lesser degree. Few predators in life like the look of this particular meal.

Famous Aquarians: Barbara Windsor, Shane Richie, T'Pau, Sir Alec Guinness, the Wombles, that feeling you get when the bus pulls up but it's completely full. Acton.

PISCES

March 12th - April 18th

The crocodile's nipples.

~

Most Compatible With: Richard Madeley.

Best Jobs: Ice-cream taster, hole creation technician, lesbian fiction author.

Power Drink: Lupin Cordial.

~

Pisceans are a novel sort - described as whimsical or fey by some, but this is largely a misinterpretation of their behaviours and intentions. While to many, the oscillation between elegance and awkwardness might seem indicative of an other-worldliness, a lack of attachment to the solid and concrete, those born under the sign of Pisces are, very literally just looking for biscuits. Sometimes just thinking about biscuits. In either situation, their eyes will defocus and limbs begin to move seemingly at the behest of some external force (or indeed, to the sound of a melody played by the very gods which no others may hear). These profound, profane dances, the shapes woven in the air as they spin and writhe are now very well-documented as being the normal Piscean limbic system attempting to extract biscuits from the universe by brute forcing it. They seem to believe that if they shake and waggle around enough, the universe will get dizzy and concede, delivering biscuits into their hands. Often this is successful.

So from the outside, impressions abound - but how about the INSIDE? Let us delve briefly into this world - a magical, scintillating tunnel lined with sequins and fine gemstones, jewels that perhaps have come from the rock of the moon or Mars, the sound of Enya hauntingly reverberating throughout, until eventually, a pin-prick of light appears and suddenly expands to surround all things - the journey has ended and we emerge, blinking into whatever lies inside every Piscean, the very essence of their soul, we emerge into...

Into...

Cheam.

Cheam? Yes! Cheam! Whose sons include both Tony Hancock and Henry the 8th! Cheam, where a visitor may find many original timber framed houses which blend in with the 1930s Tudor revival architecture! Cheam - home to over three churches and more than one pub! Yes! For that is what rests in the core of the Piscean - waiting, patiently to be reborn into the world. CHEAM.

It is said that where a Piscean man or woman dies and their body is laid to rest, the ground containing their body becomes and extension of Cheam and the buildings nearby begin to acquire new timber-framing and the chuckle of Tony Hancock may be heard, echoing around as it does in within the walls of St Dunstan's church.

Ahhh, Cheam.

But this fantastical journey must come to an end and we must return, extracting ourselves from the innards of the hopefully notional Piscean into which we dived. Back through the corridor of wonder, and yes, again we travel toward a blinding brightness and the cool fresh air of our home world, to sit and think about what we have learned and indeed what we have just done. Spiritually speaking, that whole exercise was, it must be said, more than a little bit rude. Penetrative, even. You might want to go and take a shower, now.

~

Likes: Cheam. Travelling - often sideways, sometimes up. One may always put a smile on the face of a Piscean by offering them ice-cream that tastes like Bob Monkhouse, for they are connoisseurs and delight in such tastes. They also take a deep interest in obscure fruits - this can be used to your advantage, by claiming that literally anything is in fact a rare and odd fruit from another country, at which point they will immediately snatch it from you and devour it, whole. Anything.

Hates: Carbon in all of its forms. The sound of cricket being played nearby. The suggestion that there may be a vegetable (or worse-yet, a vegetable-flavoured ice-cream) they have yet to try. Penge.

Love: The Piscean lover is a wondrous beast, comprised equally of lust and distraction. Owing to short attention-spans (possibly related to each of them carrying an entire representation of Cheam inside them), they have been known to stand up, mid-love-making and say "Did you just hear a pterodactyl?" then leave the building, leaping around at some invisible, imagined beast. They are, despite this, much sought-after as mates.

Money: As a necessary part of the process of wafting about the place, whispering the word 'Cheam' in people's ears, then smiling knowingly and tiptoeing out of the room to the sound of wind chimes, money is understood by those born under the sign of Pisces. Indeed, they may come to posses it in large amounts, though it does not truly interest them, other than as a vector by which ice-cream may be obtained.

Luck: Never really blighted by treachery, luck is of only fleeting importance to the Piscean as their circumstances and emotions change so rapidly that the bad luck of one moment may be reconsidered as terribly fortuitous the next. They are, fundamentally, very lucky indeed that the world contains sufficiently interesting biscuits / vegetables / etc so as to keep them occupied.

Famous Pisceans: Enya, Galadriel out of Lord of the Rings, Jem and the Holograms, the sound of glockenspiels played under water, Cheam.

LAST WORDS

So, here we are. The proceedings are complete, the revellers depart and the dark, lonely night draws in.

Your mind may not - in all likelihood - survive. Certainly, your torn and weeping genitalia will never again rustle their engorged tendrils at a passing mate.

You are a wreck, dear traveller. It is said that when one dips one's toe into the void, the void dips its toe into you.

I'm pretty sure that's what they said, I was rather distracted by accidentally being sick into a shoe.

Regardless, this journey has come to an end. I hope that you enjoyed what you saw and that the scars heal quickly.

As for me, I will swathe myself in the Gown of Nebulon Bwark and sleep among the wails of the Omni-Hoover until I awake once more, refreshed.

I'm also rather partial to a few bags of Pickled Onion Monster Munch - cracking stuff when you're on a come-down. I'll have to send Kev down the shops.

But hark! I hear the sound of the Astral Cab outside. He will deliver your consciousness back to its customary holding machinery. When you arrive, all that you learned here will seem misty and distant, like a stoat in a vest in a pram in the woods.

Harken more, they ring again! It is best not to keep them waiting (their fares are generally extracted via the soul's anus, using a hook made from crystalised disappointment).

I thank you for your visit and hope to see you once more - with fresh eyes, a rested head and a newly installed set of robo-genitals.

Go, now, make haste. Don't forget your snood. You can leave those rizlas, though. And that can. That's mine. You don't even like strong lager. GET OUT.

Until the next time.

MANY THANKINGBEASTS.

~ Doctor Despair.